Discovery

Foundation edition

GU00862589

Discovery

PHILOSOPHY & ETHICS FOR OCR GCSE RELIGIOUS STUDIES

Foundation edition

Jon Mayled
Libby Ahluwalia

Text © Jon Mayled and Libby Ahluwalia 2003

Original illustrations © Nelson Thornes Ltd 2003

The right of Jon Mayled and Libby Ahluwalia to be identified as authors of this work has been asserted by them in accordance with the Copyright, Designs and Patents Act 1988.

All rights reserved. No part of this publication may be reproduced or transmitted in any form or by any means, electronic or mechanical, including photocopy, recording or any information storage and retrieval system, without permission in writing from the publisher or under licence from the Copyright Licensing Agency Limited, of 90 Tottenham Court Road, London W1T 4LP.

Any person who commits any unauthorised act in relation to this publication may be liable to criminal prosecution and civil claims for damages.

Published in 2003 by:
Nelson Thornes Ltd
Delta Place
27 Bath Road
CHELTENHAM
GL53 7TH
United Kingdom

05 06 07 / 10 9 8 7 6 5 4 3 2

A catalogue record for this book is available from the British Library

ISBN 0 7487 7157 3

Edited by Katherine James

Page make-up by DC Graphic Design Ltd

Printed and bound in China by Midas Printing International Ltd

Contents

Introduction

This book has been written especially to cover the content and skill of the OCR GCSE Religious Studies specifications B 1931 (full course) and 1031 (short course) Philosophy and Ethics. However, it is also suitable for use with some of the specifications of other awarding bodies.

The entire content of the course for each of the ten units and each of the four religions available is covered by the text.

In order to make the text more accessible for students, the strict specification order is not necessarily followed within each Topic. Teachers should also note that the sub-headings within the Topics, although following those of the specification, have also been simplified.

Where it is helpful for all students to have general background information about a Topic, this is provided in an introductory spread, before the religion-specific content.

A number of conventions have been adopted in this text. All spellings conform to the SCAA Glossary of Religious Terms 1994. The sacred texts used for quotations are those used by OCR in examination papers:

Holy Bible New International Version, International Bible Society, Colorado, 0-340-56782-1

The Stone Edition Tanach, Mesorah Publications, 0-88906-269-5

The Meaning of the Holy Qur'an, Ali, Amana Publications, 0951595755-8

Hindu Scriptures, Zaehner, Everyman, 1-85715-064-3

The transliteration of Arabic words in the text is based on the SCAA Glossary 1994 and 'A Popular Dictionary of Islam', I R Netton, Curzon Press, London, 1992, 0 7007 0233 4. The Arabic letters *ay* and *hamza* are transliterated throughout as ' and ' respectively.

In the Jewish scriptures, G-d's name is spelt with four consonants YHWH (this is called the **Tetragrammaton** or 'four letters'), but Jewish teaching says that the name is so holy that only the High Priest knew how to pronounce it and that he only spoke it once a year, alone, in the Holy of Holies in the Temple at Jerusalem.

When they see these four letters Jews usually say the name **Adonai** instead – this means Lord. Many Jews will not write the word that is a translation of this name and instead put G-d. In some parts of the **Tenakh** the name HASHEM is also used for G-d.

In Islam Muslims use the words '**Salla-llahu alaihi wa sallam**' – peace and blessings of Allah upon him – every time the Prophet Muhammad ﷺ is mentioned. Similar respect is accorded to the other Prophets. The Arabic colophon ﷺ in the text represents these words.

This Foundation edition has been prepared so that it can be used alongside the mainstream edition of *Discovery*. The text has been simplified where possible whilst all the essential material has been retained. Keywords have been emboldened and a list of glossary words is included at the end of each relevant spread.

UNIT 1

The Nature of God

Christianity

Christian beliefs about the nature of God

Christians believe there is only one God. They believe that God is not like anything else, so it can be very difficult to find the words to explain beliefs about God. God is often described as 'holy', which means special, separate and different.

Christians believe:
● God is eternal, which means outside time and space. God is everywhere at all times.
● God made the world and everything in it. God has a plan for the world.
● God is good and loving. God is perfect.
● God cares how people behave and how they treat each other.
● God is all-powerful (omnipotent) and all-knowing (omniscient).
● God will judge each person.

The doctrine of the Trinity

One of the ways that Christians try to explain their beliefs about God is called the **doctrine of the Trinity**. They say God can be understood in three different ways: as God the Father, as God the Son, and as God the Holy Spirit. This does not mean there are three different gods. It means that God relates to people in different ways.

God the Father
Calling God 'Father' is a way of showing belief that God made everything. It is also a way of showing belief that God loves people as a good father loves his children. Some Christians also talk about God as 'Mother', to show that God is not just male or female.

God the Son
Christians believe that Jesus of Nazareth was the Son of God. They believe that when Jesus was born, God chose to come to earth as a man. He taught people the right way to live. He showed them what life will be like when God rules (the **kingdom of God**, or **kingdom of heaven**). He died on the cross so that people could be forgiven for doing wrong. They believe that after Jesus died, he rose from the dead (the **resurrection**) and showed that God has power over death.

God the Holy Spirit
Christians believe that after Jesus rose from the dead, he went back into heaven (the **ascension**). God sent the Holy Spirit into the lives of Christians, giving them courage and helping them. In Christian art, the Holy Spirit is often shown as a dove, a symbol of peace and hope.

Christians believe that Jesus was the Son of God, and that when he was baptised, the Holy Spirit came down on him like a dove.

Why do Christians believe in God?

Christians give many reasons for believing in God. They might say:

● Nothing happens without a reason. The universe cannot have just started by itself, by accident. It must have been made, by God.

● Everything in the world seems to be carefully designed to do different things. There must be a God who designed it all.

● We all have a sense of right and wrong. We feel guilty when we do wrong even if we know no-one will find out. There must be a God who gives us a sense of right and wrong.

● Some people feel they have met with God in a special way, perhaps as an answer to prayer, or a healing, or a strong feeling that God is with them.

● Some people are brought up in a Christian family, and Christianity has always been part of their lives.

Many people might argue that these are not good reasons for belief in God. They might say that the universe could have happened by accident. It could be the result of a 'Big Bang', not God. Or they might say that evolution, not God, designed the animals and plants to do different things. Some people say that our sense of right and wrong comes from the way we were brought up by our parents, not from God. They might say that coming from a Christian family does not show Christianity is true. They might say that someone who has felt God is near them might have made a mistake.

No-one can prove that God exists; but no-one can prove that there is no God, either.

Discussion

Do you think that Christianity provides good reasons for belief in God? Explain why, or why not.

Activity

1 Make a list of some of the different words Christians use to describe God, such as *omnipotent* and *loving*.

2 Christians use the doctrine of the Trinity to explain some of their beliefs about God. In your own words, explain what Christians mean by each of:
God the Father
God the Son
God the Holy Spirit.

Glossary words

doctrine of the Trinity

kingdom of God/kingdom of heaven

resurrection

ascension

The authority of the Bible for Christians

The Bible is the holy book of Christianity. It is in two sections: the Old Testament, and the New Testament.

The **Old Testament** is the same as the holy writings of the Jews. It contains 39 books of stories, poems, laws, history, myths, prophecy and songs. The books are about God and how God deals with different people over hundreds of years.

The **New Testament** contains 27 books. There are four **gospels** which tell the story of the life, teaching, death and rising back to life of Jesus. There are also other books containing history, letters to new Christians, and writing about the future end of the world. For many Christians, the New Testament is even more special than the Old Testament because it contains the story of Jesus and gives a new understanding of God.

Christians believe that the Bible comes from God. They try to understand its teachings and put them into practice every day. They read about people who are praised in the Bible, and they try to behave in the same way themselves. They look to the Bible for teaching about moral issues, to help them decide what choices to make. The Bible has *authority* for Christians, which means that they believe it is something they should respect and obey.

Different ways of understanding the Bible

Christians have different ideas about how to understand the Bible. Some think that the stories in the Bible all really happened exactly as described. If other people say the Bible is wrong, then they should not be believed, because God does not make mistakes. Science or history comes from people, who do make mistakes, but the Bible is always right.

Other Christians believe that there are different kinds of truth in the Bible. They say that some of the stories are myths, which give true messages but do not always describe real events. They also say that people wrote the Bible. The ideas came from God, but the people who wrote them down might sometimes have used their own ideas too and made some mistakes.

All Christians believe that the Bible is very special, and more important than any other book. They read the Bible in church services on Sundays. They read it at special times such as weddings and funerals. Many Christians read the Bible on their own at home or in small groups with other Christians.

God in the world

Christians believe that God did not just start off the world and then go away. They believe that God is interested in each person and that God takes part in the things that happen in the world.

Miracles

Many Christians believe that God acts in the world by doing miracles. Some people believe they have been healed by miracles, even from illnesses that usually have no cure. In the Bible, there are many stories of Jesus doing miracles. For example, in Luke's gospel there is the story of a blind beggar, who was given back his sight:

> He asked him, 'What do you want me to do for you?' He said, 'Lord, let me see again.' Jesus said to him, 'Receive your sight; your faith has saved you.' Immediately he regained his sight.
>
> (Luke 18:41–42)

Christians believe that miracles still happen today. Lourdes is a place where Roman Catholics go as pilgrims, because they believe that the Virgin Mary

Christians believe that God sometimes works through miracles. Some visit Lourdes in the hope of being cured by a miracle.

appeared there in a vision. When they visit Lourdes, they often go in the hope that God will perform a miracle there.

Jesus

For Christians, the most important way that God showed care for the world was when he came to earth as Jesus Christ. The writer of John's gospel puts it like this:

> And the Word became flesh and lived among us, and we have seen his glory, the glory as of a father's only son, full of grace and truth.
>
> (John 1:14)

Christians believe that we do not have to wonder what God is like, because God came into the world and showed us. They say that because God came into the world, it shows that God cares enough about people to want to teach them things, and to share with them the happy and sad parts of human life.

Discussion

Do you think miracles happen today? If someone told you that he or she had seen a miracle, would you believe it? Explain why, or why not.

Activity

1 Explain why Christians believe the Bible is special.

2 Describe how Christians might use the Bible in their daily lives.

3 Christians say they believe God does miracles. Give some examples of events that might be called 'miracles'.

Glossary words

Old Testament

New Testament

gospels

Hinduism

Hindu beliefs about the nature of God

In Hinduism, there are many different beliefs about God, and some Hindus do not believe in God at all. Many Hindus believe that there is only one God, but others believe that there are many different gods and goddesses.

The gods and goddesses are known as **deities**. They are all different.

- **Shiva** is often called the 'lord of the dance'. He dances in a circle of flame, which shows the endless circle of life. He is the deity who makes things and destroys things.
- **Ganesha** is a god with an elephant's head. He helps people and is a god of good luck. He gives special help to young people in their education.
- **Lakshmi** is a goddess of beauty and of money. She is often a favourite with people who have their own business.

Ganesha is one of the deities of Hinduism, always shown with an elephant's head.

- **Rama** and **Sita** are the heroes of a long story called the **Ramayana**. They are seen as good examples of how married couples should behave.

Brahman

Most Hindus believe in many gods. Many Hindus also believe that behind it all, there is only one God. All the different deities are different ways of understanding this same God. This one God is called **Brahman**. Hindus might say that people cannot understand God all at once, because it is too big an idea for the human mind. Having different deities is a way of looking at God from different angles, to try and understand God better.

Brahman, the one God, is usually divided into three main parts: the gods Brahma, Shiva and Vishnu.

Most Hindus believe that God is in everything: beginnings and ends, male and female, good and evil, movement and stillness. God is also present in every person, as an eternal spirit called **Atman**.

Why do Hindus believe in God?

Hindus who believe in God give many different reasons for their beliefs.

- Some Hindus talk about their own personal feelings of being with God. Hindus pray and meditate as part of their worship, and some believe that they have met with God in this way.
- Hindus might say that because the universe is here, and everything in the universe fits together, it shows that everything is part of God.
- Many Hindus have their beliefs because it is part of their culture, and the way they have been taught by their parents.

Some religions try hard to make others believe in God, and they give reasons to support their beliefs. Hinduism is not like this. In Hinduism there are many different ways of understanding the world. Hindus think that people with all different beliefs should be able to live together.

Hindu sacred writings

The Vedas

Hinduism has many sacred writings (holy books), written in the holy language of **Sanskrit**. The oldest and most important are called the **Vedas**. These are known as **sruti,** which means 'that which is heard'. Other less important books are called **smriti**, 'that which is remembered'.

Hindus believe that the Vedas were not written by any human being, but were heard by wise people called **rishis** and have been repeated ever since. The Vedas did not begin as written books. They were spoken words passed on from the old people to the young, and they were only put into writing many hundreds of years later.

Most Hindus have not read the Vedas for themselves. They know some of the words because they have heard them repeated during worship and at special times such as weddings.

The Vedas contain hymns, myths, songs, chants, and prayers. They tell stories of the gods, and raise questions which people have been asking since the beginning. How did the world begin? Can people live for ever? What is wisdom, and where can it be found?

Other sacred writings

The **Upanishads** are also very important writings for Hindus. The name 'Upanishad' means 'sitting at the feet of the teacher'. The Upanishads explain discussions between religious teachers (**gurus**) and their students.

The **Bhagavad Gita** is another sacred text which is very much loved by Hindus. It is part of a long story known as the Mahabharata. The Bhagavad Gita tells the story of the god Krishna and a warrior called Arjuna. Krishna teaches Arjuna about why it is important to do his duty. He shows Arjuna a vision of God.

Hindu holy books tell many stories. The important ideas are usually taught by speaking and listening, not by reading. The words are said during worship so that 'that which is heard' and 'that which is remembered' can go on being heard and remembered by future generations.

Discussion

What do you think might be the good points and bad points of passing on religious ideas and stories by word of mouth rather than by writing them down?

Activity

1 Explain what Hindus mean when they say that there is one God who can be worshipped in different ways.

2 Why are the Vedas believed to be more important than other Hindu books?

3 Describe how Hindu holy books are usually used.

Glossary words

deities	Vedas
Shiva	Sanskrit
Ganesha	sruti
Lakshmi	smriti
Rama	rishis
Sita	Upanishads
Ramayana	gurus
Brahman	Bhagavad Gita
Atman	

Avatars

Hindus believe that sometimes, a god will come to earth, in the form of a person or animal. These are known as **avatars**. Avatars appear at times of danger.

Hindus believe that the god Vishnu came to earth as an avatar.

1 The first avatar was in the form of a fish. Vishnu appeared to save a great teacher called Manu from a flood. There was the danger that his holy books would be lost.

2 Vishnu appeared as a giant tortoise. The gods had lost their holy drink **amrit**. The tortoise helped the gods to get the amrit back from the bottom of the sea, using his curved shell.

3 The earth was in danger from being sent to the bottom of the ocean by a demon. Vishnu appeared as a boar and used his tusks to keep the earth above water.

4 Vishnu appeared as half lion, half man. He came to kill an evil demon. Vishnu killed him by tearing him to pieces.

5 The fifth avatar was Vishnu in the form of a dwarf. A demon told him he could have only as much land as he could cover in three steps. Vishnu turned into a giant and covered the whole earth in three steps. He stamped on the evil demon and the demon was killed.

6 Once, the Kshatriyas, who are the warrior group in Hinduism, said they would take over from the Brahmins, who are the priests. Vishnu became 'Rama with the axe' and kept Hindu society organised in the way it was meant to be.

7 The seventh avatar of Vishnu, called Rama, is one of the most popular characters in Hinduism. His story is told in the Ramayana.

Rama the prince should have become king, but his jealous stepmother wanted the throne to go to her own son. Rama was sent away to live in the forest, with Rama's faithful wife, Sita, and his loyal younger brother Lakshmana. They lived in the forest for fourteen years. When Rama and

Rama, as an avatar of Vishnu, defeated the many-headed demon Ravanna.

Lakshmana were off hunting, a demon kidnapped Sita. Rama and Lakshmana had many adventures while they were looking for Sita. In the end, Rama and Lakshmana were helped by Hanuman, the monkey god. They found Sita and rescued her, and they destroyed Ravanna, the evil demon.

Rama and Sita are popular gods for Hindus. They give an example of how a husband and wife should be.

8 The eighth avatar of Vishnu was Krishna. He is also a very popular god. Krishna is shown as young, blue in colour, and playing on his flute. There are many stories about Krishna as a child. He was always up to tricks but had special powers. As he grew up, he was a great favourite with the young

women called gopis who looked after the cows and goats. The gopi who loved Krishna most was called Radha.

Krishna is a very popular Hindu deity, often shown playing a flute.

Krishna is also worshipped as a great teacher. In the Hindu book called the Bhagavad Gita, Krishna appeared at a battle to teach the right way to live.

9 The ninth avatar was Siddharta Gautama the Buddha, the leader of Buddhism. He taught that it was important not to be greedy for possessions, and about the need to avoid doing any harm (**ahimsa**).

Hindus believe that the tenth avatar of Vishnu has not yet come. When there is another need for Vishnu to fight evil, he will come again in the form of Kalki, carrying a flashing sword and riding a white horse.

Hindus believe God does not just come to the earth from time to time. They think God is in people's lives every day. Hindus will pray to different deities and ask for their help; for example, they might pray to Lord Ganesha and ask him to help their children at school. They might pray to the goddess Lakshmi if they needed help with money problems. They believe that God will help them.

Discussion

If you asked Hindus whether they believed in one god, or many gods, what do you think they would say?

Activity

1 What is an avatar?

2 What do Hindus believe about Rama?

3 What do Hindus believe about Krishna?

Glossary words

avatars

amrit

ahimsa

Muslim beliefs about the nature of Allah

Muslims believe there is only one God – Allah. Allah is not like anything else that exists and Muslims do not try to describe him.

Muslims believe:
- Allah is eternal, beyond time and space.
- Allah does not have a physical body, and is everywhere at all times.
- Allah created the world and everything in it, and has a purpose for the world.
- Allah is perfectly good and perfectly loving.
- Allah is interested in how people behave, and wants them to treat each other properly.
- Allah is all-powerful and all-knowing.
- Allah will judge everyone.

Islam means 'submission' and Muslim life is submission to the will of Allah. People live by the words of the **Qur'an** and follow the teaching and example of Muhammad ﷺ.

The importance of Allah to Muslim life is stressed in the first **Surah** of the Qur'an:

> In the name of Allah, Most Gracious, Most Merciful. Praise be to Allah, the Cherisher and Sustainer of the Worlds.
>
> (Surah 1)

The **Shahadah** is the first pillar of Islam and the main statement of belief. It says why Allah is important.

> *La ilaha illal lahu Muhammad Dur rasulul lah*
>
> There is no god but Allah, Muhammad ﷺ is the messenger of Allah.

This is repeated in **Salah**, daily prayers.

The **Adhan**, or call to prayer, has the following statements:

Allah is the Greatest (x 4)
I bear witness that there is no god but Allah (x 2)

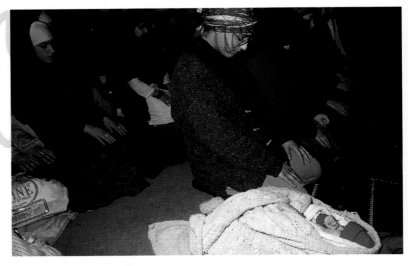

I bear witness that Muhammad is Allah's messenger (x 2)
Rush to prayer (x 2)
Rush to success (x 2)
Allah is the Greatest (x 2)
There is no god but Allah

Prayer five times a day is a very important part of Muslim life

Al-Imanul Mufassal states the seven basic beliefs:

> I believe in Allah, in His angels, in His books, in His messengers, in the Last Day and in the fact that everything good or bad is decided by Allah, the Almighty, and in the Life after Death.

Tawhid – Allah is 'one' – is stated in the Qur'an and is the most important part of what Muslims believe:

> Say: He is Allah, the One and Only; Allah, the Eternal, Absolute; He begetteth not, nor is He begotten; and there is none like unto Him.
>
> (Surah 112:1–4)

Muslims try to let Tawhid shape and control the whole of their lives. In this way they become contented. They trust in Allah and dedicate their lives to give him pleasure.

Muslims have collected the 99 'most beautiful names' of God, and these are often used in meditation.

Tradition says that the hundredth name is a secret, known only to the camel. Muhammad ﷺ said:

> There are ninety-nine names that are Allah's alone. Whoever learns, understands and enumerates them enters Paradise and achieves eternal salvation.

These principles of Muslim belief can all be found in the last sermon which Muhammad ﷺ preached on Mount Arafat at the end of the **Hajj**:

> O people, listen to my words carefully, for I know not whether I would meet you again on such an occasion.
>
> O people, just as you regard this month, this day, this city as sacred, so regard the lip and property of every Muslim as a sacred trust. Remember that you will indeed appear before Allah and answer for your actions...
>
> O people, listen carefully! All the believers are brothers...
>
> O people, none is higher than the other unless he is higher in obedience to Allah. No Arab is superior to a non-Arab except in piety.
>
> O people, reflect on my words. I leave behind me two things, the Qur'an and my example, and if you follow these, you will not fail.
>
> Listen to me carefully! Worship Allah and offer Salah, observe Saum in the month of Ramadan and pay Zakah...
>
> O people, no prophet or messenger will come after me and no new faith will emerge.
>
> All those who listen to me shall pass on my words to others, and those to others again.
>
> (Hadith)

Why do Muslims believe in Allah?

Muslims believe in Allah because they see how good he is when they look at their daily lives and the world around them. They also believe in him because he revealed the Qur'an to Muhammad ﷺ.

Muslims believe that Allah has already decided what will happen to everyone in the world. This is called **Al-Qadr**. Humans are Allah's agents on earth. They can choose to disobey Allah but if they do they will be judged at **Akhirah**, the day of judgement.

Allah can 'speak' to people by **Risalah** – the Prophets. According to Muhammad ﷺ there are 124,000 prophets but only 25 are mentioned in the Qur'an. Many of these prophets are the same people as are found in the Jewish and Christian scriptures. This shows part of the common roots of these three religions.

Muhammad ﷺ was the last prophet and received the final revelation from Allah. He is sometimes called the 'Seal of the Prophets'.

Discussion

Do you think that Islam sets out good reasons for belief in Allah? Explain why, or why not.

Activity

Write a sentence in your own words about each of these words: *Allah, Risalah, Shahadah*.

Glossary words

Islam

Qur'an

Surah

Shahadah

Salah

Adhan

Hajj

Al-Qadr

Akhirah

Risalah

Muslim sacred writings

The Qur'an is the holy book of Islam. Muslims believe it was revealed by God – that it records Allah's words. The Qur'an mentions other books which were also revealed by God: Zabur (Psalms of David), Tawrat (Torah of Moses), Injil (Gospels of the New Testament), Suhuf-i-Ibrahim (Scrolls of Abraham). Islam says that only the Qur'an is still in its original form and that these other books have been changed from the original words of God.

The Qur'an is, in some ways, very different from the holy books of Judaism and Christianity.

Muslims say that the Qur'an was revealed to Muhammad ﷺ by the angel Jibril and is the actual words of Allah.

In 611 CE, Muhammad ﷺ, then aged 40, was meditating in a cave. Jibril appeared to him and ordered him to read. Muhammad ﷺ said that he could not read. This happened three times and eventually the angel said:

> Proclaim! (or read) in the name of thy Lord and Cherisher, Who created – created man, out of a (mere) clot of congealed blood. Proclaim! And thy Lord is Most Bountiful – He Who has taught (the use of) the Pen – taught man that which he knew not.
>
> (Surah 96:1–5)

Muhammad ﷺ recited these words and then the angel said, 'O Muhammad, you are the messenger of Allah and I am Jibril', and left.

Muhammad ﷺ received more visits from Jibril over the next 23 years. Just before his death, he received the final verse:

> This day have I perfected your religion for your benefit, completed My favour upon you, and have chosen for you Islam as your religion.
>
> (Surah 5:3)

Muhammad ﷺ could not read or write, so he repeated the words to his secretary,

Zaid Bin Thabit. They were not put together as a book until after his death.

Every copy of the Qur'an has the words of Allah just as they were received by Muhammad ﷺ. Because of this, versions of the Qur'an in languages other than Arabic are not called translations. Muslims say it is not possible to translate God's words into any other language without changing them.

The Qur'an is not written in the order of the events which it contains. Surah 1 is the shortest and is then followed by the longest Surah. The Surahs then grow progressively shorter until the last which is 114.

No-one criticises the Qur'an because it is the word of Allah. There is no point in discussing who wrote it and why, because it all comes from Allah.

The Qur'an cannot be changed and does not change. It is the complete and final book of guidance from Allah for the whole of humanity forever.

The Qur'an and the teachings of Islam are regarded as absolute truth. Muslims say that they do not have to believe because they actually know these teachings to be true.

The cave on Mount Nur where Jibril spoke to Muhammad ﷺ.

Allah in the world

Miracles are not very important in Islam. Muhammad ﷺ was a prophet, not a god, so there is no reason why he should have performed miracles.

Allah, of course, can perform miracles. There were many times in the life of Muhammad ﷺ when Allah intervened.

One story is about Muhammad's ﷺ birth. On the night that he was born a great star appeared in the sky. His grandfather Abd al-Muttalib prayed for six days to decide on a name for the child. On the seventh day both he and Muhammad's ﷺ mother dreamt that he should be called Muhammad ﷺ – the 'Praised One'.

The most important miracle in the life of the Prophet was **Al-Mi'raj** – the Ascent. Muslims believe that Muhammad ﷺ was woken by Jibril who took him to Jerusalem, riding on an animal with wings, called Buraq. In Jerusalem Muhammad ﷺ met the prophets Adam, Ibrahim, Musa, 'Isa and Harun and he then travelled through the heavens until he came before Allah.

By choosing Muhammad ﷺ and revealing the Qur'an to him, Allah ensured the future of Islam. This revelation can be seen as the greatest miracle.

Discussion

Do you think that an event like the revelation of the Qur'an could still happen today? Give reasons to support your answer.

Activity

1 What do Muslims mean when they say that the Qur'an is revealed?

2 Describe how Muslims might use the Qur'an in their daily lives.

Glossary words

Al-Mi'raj

Judaism

Jewish beliefs about the nature of G-d

In the Jewish scriptures, G-d's name is spelt with four consonants YHWH. Jews say that the name is so holy that only the High Priest knew how to pronounce it and that he only spoke it once a year, alone, in the Temple at Jerusalem. When they see these four letters Jews usually say the name **Adonai** instead – this means Lord. Many Jews will not write the word that is a translation of this name and instead put G-d. In some parts of the Jewish scriptures the name **HASHEM** is also used for G-d.

Jews believe there is only one G-d. G-d is not like anything else and this means that it is very difficult to describe G-d. G-d is often described as 'holy', which means special, separate and different.

Jews believe:
● G-d is eternal, beyond time and space.
● G-d does not have a physical body, and is everywhere at all times.
● G-d is the creator of the world and everything in it, and has a purpose for the world.
● G-d is perfectly good and perfectly loving.
● G-d is interested in how people behave, and wants them to treat each other properly.
● G-d is all-powerful (omnipotent) and all-knowing (omniscient).
● G-d judges everyone.

Genesis, the first book of the Jewish Scriptures, begins with a description of G-d creating the world:

> In the beginning of G-d's creating the heavens and the earth – when the earth was astonishingly empty, with darkness upon the surface of the deep, and the Divine Presence hovered upon the surface of the waters – G-d said, 'Let there be light', and there was light.
>
> (Genesis 1:1–2)

G-d speaks to Moses through a bush which is burning and Moses asks G-d's name:

> HASHEM answered Moses, 'I SHALL BE AS I SHALL BE.'
>
> (Exodus 3:14)

The Jewish scriptures say that Moses spoke to G-d:

> As Moses would arrive at the Tent, the pillar of cloud would descend and stand at the entrance of the Tent, and He would speak with Moses... HASHEM would speak to Moses face to face, as a man would speak with his fellow.
>
> (Exodus 33:9, 11)

The Torah scrolls, the most sacred Jewish scriptures, are kept in the ark. The art is the holiest part of the synagogue.

Later, when Moses was receiving the Ten Commandments, he asked to see G-d:

> He said, 'I will make all My goodness pass before you, and I shall call out with the Name, HASHEM before you…' He said, 'You will not be able to see My face, for no human can see My face and live!' HASHEM said, 'Behold! there is a place near Me; you may stand on the rock. When My glory passes by, I shall place you in a cleft of the rock; I shall shield you with My hand until I have passed. Then I shall remove My hand and you will see My back, but My face may not be seen.'
>
> (Exodus 33:19–23)

Only in the Garden of Eden does G-d appear in a human form:

> So G-d created Man in His image, in the image of G-d He created him; male and female He created them.
>
> (Genesis 1:27)

> They heard the sound of HASHEM G-d manifesting itself in the garden toward the evening.
>
> (Genesis 3:8)

G-d is sometimes a pillar of cloud or flame, and sometimes just a voice:

> [The word of G-d] then said, 'Go out [of the cave] and stand on the mountain before HASHEM.' And behold, HASHEM was passing, and a great, powerful wind, smashing mountains and breaking rocks, went before HASHEM. 'HASHEM is not in the wind' [Elijah was told]. After the wind came an earthquake. 'HASHEM is not in the earthquake!' After the earthquake came a fire. 'HASHEM is not in the fire!' After the fire came a still, thin sound.
>
> (1 Kings 19:11–12)

On other occasions G-d is shown as a powerful king:

> …I saw the Lord sitting upon a high and lofty throne, and its legs filled the Temple. Seraphim were standing above, at His service. Each one had six wings… And one would call to another and say,
>
> 'Holy, holy, holy is HASHEM, Master of Legions; the whole world is filled with His glory.'
>
> The doorposts moved many cubits at the sound of the calling, and the Temple became filled with smoke.
>
> (Isaiah 6:1–4)

Discussion

Do you think that Judaism provides convincing reasons for belief in God? Explain why, or why not.

Activity

1 Why do Jews write *G-d?*

2 Why do Jews find it difficult to describe G-d?

Glossary words

Adonai

HASHEM

Reasons Jews give in support of their belief in G-d

Jews believe that there is only one G-d. This belief is in the **Shema**, a very important prayer in Judaism. Belief in one G-d is at the centre of Jewish life.

> Hear, O Israel: HASHEM is our G-d, HASHEM is the One and Only. You shall love HASHEM, your G-d, with all your heart, with all your soul, and with all your resources. And these matters that I command you today shall be upon your heart. You shall teach them thoroughly to your children and you shall speak of them while you sit in your home, while you walk on the way, when you retire and when you arise. Bind them as a sign upon your arm and let them be ornaments between your eyes. And write them on the doorposts of your house and upon your gates.
>
> (Deuteronomy 6:4–9)

The covenant

Judaism teaches that Abraham entered into a special relationship with G-d called a **covenant**. This was an agreement between them that Abraham and his family would worship this one G-d and no others, and that G-d would look after his family and descendants forever.

The authority for Jews of the Torah and Talmud

The **Torah** (Law) is very important to Jews. It contains five books which, in English, are called Genesis, Exodus, Leviticus, Numbers and Deuteronomy.

The Torah is the first part of the **Tenakh**. The other two parts are the **Ketuvim** (Writings) which contains 11 books and the **Nevi'im** (Prophets) which has 16 books.

Judaism teaches that the five books of the Torah were all written by Moses, who was told what to write by G-d – so they are revealed. Jews do not all believe that every word in the Torah has to be true. For example, the story of Creation and of Adam and Eve may not be historical fact, but it does contain important teachings about G-d and about human nature.

The Torah is treated with great respect by all Jews. It is handwritten by a scribe on large pages made of animal skin and is placed on large rollers. These **scrolls** are decorated with covers and hung with bells and other decorations. When they are not in use the scrolls are kept in a cupboard in the synagogue called the **aron hakodesh** (the ark). When they are being read they are not touched by hand but a **yad** (pointer) is used so that the reader can follow the text.

Jews also have the **Talmud**, or 'Oral Torah', to help them understand the five books of the Torah (the 'Written Torah'). Jews believe that the Oral Torah was given to Moses at the same time as G-d gave him the Written Torah. The Oral Torah helps to explain the text of the Written Torah. The Talmud is a collection of the teachings and explanations of rabbis.

The respect which Jews give to the Torah and the **mitzvot** (laws) shows how important they are to them.

Tefillin are worn at prayertime. They contain scrolls on which are written the words of the Shema.

A silver pointer called a yad is used to follow the text so that it is not touched by hand.

The Bible contains the Ten Commandments (Exodus 20:1–17) but these are only ten of the 613 mitzvot (commandments) in the Torah. Jews show their belief in G-d by living according to these rules. They also live waiting for the Messiah to come, which is promised in the Torah.

Belief in G-d intervening in the world through miracles and through the words of the prophets

Miracles

There are many miracles in the Torah, for example:

- Moses and his stick which turned into a snake
- the plagues of Egypt
- the parting of the Red Sea
- the food which the Israelites were given by G-d in the desert.

If people believe these are true it means that G-d will break the physical laws

of nature in order to help humanity. While this is possible, it seems unlikely to many people, since why would G-d break the laws he has created? Many people see the stories of miracles as ways to help people understand G-d.

Prophets

Throughout the Tenakh there are prophets who warn people of what might happen if they ignore G-d's teachings. These include: Isaiah, Jeremiah, Ezekiel, Hosea, Joel, Amos, Obadiah, Jonah, Micah, Nahum, Habbakuk and Zepahaniah.

Discussion

Do you think miracles happen today? If someone told you that he or she had experienced a miracle, would you believe it? Explain why, or why not.

Activity

1 What do Jews mean when they say that the Torah is revealed?

2 How do Jews use the Torah in their daily lives?

Glossary words

Shema

covenant

Torah

Tenakh

Ketuvim

Nevi'im

scrolls

aron hakodesh

yad

Talmud

mitzvot

Christianity

(a) Describe what Christians believe about the nature of God. (8 marks)

(b) Explain how a Christian might show respect for the Bible in his or her daily life. (7 marks)

(c) 'There is no evidence that God exists.' Do you agree? Give reasons to support your answer, and show that you have thought about different points of view. You must refer to Christianity in your answer. (5 marks)

Hinduism

(a) Describe what Hindus believe about the nature of God. (8 marks)

(b) Explain how a Hindu might show respect for the Vedas in his or her daily life. (7 marks)

(c) 'There is no evidence that God exists.' Do you agree? Give reasons to support your answer, and show that you have thought about different points of view. You must refer to Hinduism in your answer. (5 marks)

Islam

(a) Describe what Muslims believe about the nature of Allah. (8 marks)

(b) Explain how a Muslim might show respect for the Qur'an in his or her daily life. (7 marks)

(c) 'There is no evidence that God exists.' Do you agree? Give reasons to support your answer, and show that you have thought about different points of view. You must refer to Islam in your answer. (5 marks)

Judaism

(a) Describe what Jews believe about the nature of G-d. (8 marks)

(b) Explain how a Jew might show respect for the Torah in his or her daily life. (7 marks)

(c) 'There is no evidence that G-d exists.' Do you agree? Give reasons to support your answer, and show that you have thought about different points of view. You must refer to Judaism in your answer. (5 marks)

Tips

For all four questions

In part **(a)**, you are asked to describe religious beliefs. You do not need to give your own opinion. You should try and allow yourself about 10–15 minutes to answer this part of the question. Try to give as much detail as you can remember, and try to use the correct terms for the beliefs. For example, if you were writing about Judaism, you might use the word 'Adonai', and if you were writing about Christianity, you could use the word 'Trinity'.

In part **(b)**, you are being tested on your understanding. You should allow about 10 minutes for this part of the question. Try to think about how the holy books might be important for the religious believer. For example, they might use words from the holy books in their prayers, or try to follow the commands as they go about their everyday lives, or use the books as a source of information. For high marks, try to think of several different ideas, and explain what you mean as clearly as you can.

In part **(c)**, you are being tested on your evaluation. This means you need to show that you realise people might have different opinions. You should explain what a religious believer might say in answer to this question. You should also show what someone of a different belief, or no belief, might say. Start by saying why a religious believer would disagree with the statement. What might they think is evidence to show that God exists? Then say why someone else might disagree with them. You also need to give your own view, and try to back it up with a reason.

UNIT 2

The Nature of Belief

Christianity

The architecture of the church

There are many different kinds of church building. Some are new and some are old, some have lots of decoration and others are very plain and simple. Many churches are built in the shape of a cross. They often have a tower or spire, which points upwards to show that Christianity is about God as well as about this world.

Near the door where people come in is the **font**. The font is used to hold water when babies are baptised. It is by the door to show that baptism is about entering the church. Not all churches have the font near the door. Some have them in the middle of

the building. In Roman Catholic churches there is also a **stoup** near the door. This holds water and people use it to make the sign of the cross as they come into the church. At the east of the church is the **altar**. This is used for Holy Communion. There is a **lectern** at the front of the church. This is a stand to rest the Bible on when someone is reading from it. The lectern is often made in the shape of an eagle, to show that the word of God is being taken across the world. The **pulpit** is a raised platform for the person who is teaching. He or she stands there to be seen and heard clearly. In Roman Catholic and Anglican churches, the altar is the most important feature of the church. Other Christians such as the Methodists give the pulpit more importance.

Christian worship

Christians worship on their own (*private* worship) and also with other people (*communal* or *corporate* worship). Both kinds of worship are important for Christians. Private worship helps Christians to think about the things that matter in their own lives. Communal or corporate worship reminds them that they are part of a group of people with the same beliefs.

Private worship

Many Christians set aside a special time of the day for private worship. They might read from the Bible. They might pray about things that are important to them, such as a friend who is ill, or something they have done wrong, or money worries, or an important event that is coming up, or something they have heard about in the news.

Many church buildings are designed in the shape of a cross, as a symbol of important Christian beliefs.

Communal worship

Most Christians belong to a church, and go to church on Sundays to worship with other people. Most church services include:

- **Hymns**, which are sung together. These are usually prayers set to music. They are a way of helping Christians to worship together when they all sing the same hymn.
- **Bible reading**, where part of the Bible is read aloud for everyone to hear and think about.
- **A sermon**, which is a talk given by the priest, minister or vicar. The sermon explains something about how to live as a Christian.
- **Prayers**, when believers can talk to God. The most famous prayer in Christianity is known as the **Lord's Prayer**, which was taught by Jesus:

Pray then in this way:

'Our Father in heaven, hallowed be your name. Your kingdom come, your will be done, on earth as it is in heaven.

Give us this day our daily bread.

And forgive us our debts, as we also have forgiven our debtors.

And do not bring us to the time of trial, but rescue us from the evil one.'

(Matthew 6:9–13)

Another popular prayer for Christians is called the Grace:

Now may the grace of our Lord Jesus Christ, and the love of God, and the fellowship of the Holy Spirit, be with us all, now and evermore. Amen.

Church services also have times of silence, for people to have their own private thoughts and prayers.

Many church services also include **Holy Communion**, or **Mass**, or the **Eucharist**. Christians share bread and wine which has been blessed as the body and blood of Christ.

Discussion

What do you think are the good points and the bad points of worshipping with a lot of other people?

Activity

Write a sentence in your own words about each of these parts of a church service: hymns, Bible reading, sermon, prayer, Holy Communion.

Glossary words

font

stoup

altar

lectern

pulpit

hymns

sermon

prayers

Lord's Prayer

Holy Communion/Mass/Eucharist

The use of food and fasting as a response to God

Christianity does not have food laws to tell Christians what they must and must not eat. Jesus probably ate meat, like other Jews. There are stories in the New Testament which tell of Jesus getting fish for hungry people:

> When he had finished speaking, he said to Simon, 'Put out into the deep water and let down your nets for a catch.' Simon answered, 'Master, we have worked all night long but have caught nothing. Yet if you say so, I will let down the nets.' When they had done this, they caught so many fish that their nets were beginning to break.
>
> (Luke 5:4–6)

Some Christians are vegetarians, but most are not. In the Acts of the Apostles, the story of the vision of Peter shows how Christians were allowed to eat all kinds of animals (Acts 10:9–16).

Food and drink in worship

Some foods, however, are used in Christian worship with a special meaning. In the Eucharist, also known as Mass, Holy Communion or the **Lord's Supper**, bread and wine are used as ways of showing Jesus living in the world. The minister, or vicar, or priest, blesses bread and wine as the body and blood of Christ. This is shared with the people. They remember the Last Supper that Jesus ate before he was crucified. When they share the bread and wine they feel they are together as Christians.

> The Lord Jesus, on the night when he was betrayed took a loaf of bread, and when he had given thanks, he broke it and said, 'This is my body that is for you. Do this in remembrance of me.' In the same way he took the cup also, after supper, saying, 'This cup is the new covenant in my blood. Do this, as often as you drink it, in remembrance of me.
>
> (1 Corinthians 11:23–25)

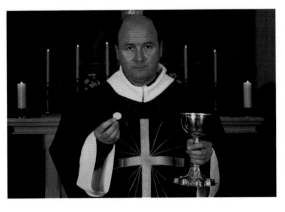

Sharing bread and wine is an important part of Christian worship.

Fasting

Fasting means going without food, and sometimes drink as well. Some people think fasting helps religious faith, because it makes people less greedy and helps them think about God. Most Christians do not fast very often, but some people choose to give up special treats during Lent (the forty days before Easter) to remind themselves of the suffering of Jesus. Monks and nuns often eat very plain food, as a way of showing that they have given their lives to God.

The use of music and art in Christian worship

Art and music have always been important in Christian worship. Some churches use a lot of art, such as paintings, carvings, needlework, stained glass and statues. Many Christians like this. They can look around the church building and remember that they are in a special place of worship. But other Christians have different views. They feel that too much art distracts people from thinking about God. The Quakers use very little art and music. They meet in simple rooms and often worship in silence.

In Christianity, music is often seen as a way of giving God the best that people can do. Hymns are used by nearly every kind of Christian church. Many churches use organ music, and some use guitars and drums.

Symbols in Christianity

The most famous and important symbol in Christianity is the cross:

This reminds Christians of the death of Jesus on a cross.

Another Christian symbol is the Chi-Rho:

This is made from two Greek letters, which are the first two letters of the word 'Christ'.

Alpha and Omega are also Greek letters:

They are at the beginning and end of the alphabet. They show that God is the beginning and end of all things.

In the earliest days of Christianity, when Christians were killed because of their beliefs, the fish was used as a secret code:

The first letters in Greek of the words 'Jesus Christ, Son of God, Saviour' spell out the Greek word for 'fish'.

Discussion

Why do you think Christianity uses symbols, and not just words?

Activity

1 (a) What is the Eucharist?

(b) Why is the Eucharist important for Christians?

2 (a) Why do some Christians like to have lots of art in their churches?

(b) Why do some other Christians prefer plain and simple church buildings?

3 Draw four of the different symbols used in Christianity. For each one, write a sentence to say what the symbol means.

Glossary words

Lord's Supper

Hinduism

Hindu worship in the home

Most Hindu worship takes place in the home. Nearly every Hindu home has its own shrine for worshipping God. In many houses, this is a corner of a room, or a special shelf, with holy pictures and objects. Some Hindus keep a whole room just for worship. Little shrines are found everywhere in Hindu countries. They are in restaurants, in cars, taxis and lorries, in shops and by the roadside. All shrines are treated as special, holy places.

The household shrine has a statue or picture of a favourite god (also known as a **deity**). This statue or picture is known as a **murti**. The murtis are always treated with great respect, because Hindus believe that God lives in them. It is the job of the woman of the house to make sure that the murtis are cared for properly. Each day, in the morning and in the evening, the murtis are worshipped. This is known as **puja**.

Before puja begins, Hindus have a bath or shower and dress in clean clothes, to show respect. Then, they say special prayers, and they ring a bell to bring God to life in the statues or pictures (murtis) in the shrine. The murti is washed and dressed in fresh clothes. The murti is brushed with coloured powders and given offerings. Sometimes Hindus meditate in silence, or say a prayer. The most popular prayer is called the **Gayatri mantra**.

Then the **arti** ceremony is performed. A special lamp with five wicks is lit and moved in a circle around the murti. Hindus pass both hands over the flame and then over their heads. This shows that they are sharing the light of God with the murti.

Hindus believe that the value of the offering to the murtis is not important. What matters is the attitude of the worshipper. In a Hindu book called the

Bhagavad Gita, the god Krishna taught that it was good to give anything, even a leaf, if it was given because of love for God.

Prayer and meditation

Bhakti is the word Hindus give for 'devotion to God'. Devotion to God in prayer is very important to Hindus. They believe it is one of the best ways of escaping from dying and being reborn over and over again.

Meditation is also important for many Hindus. Some Hindus meditate by repeating the name of God. Others try to make their minds empty and forget about things such as money and food. They try instead to feel close to God and to understand more about what really matters. Some Hindu holy men give up family life and home so that they can spend all their time meditating.

The architecture of the mandir

A Hindu temple is known as a **mandir**. Hindus do not meet together in the mandir very often, except at festivals.

The arti ceremony is an important part of Hindu worship in the home and in the mandir.

The mandir is used by people on their own and by small groups. Sometimes they take time out of the day to stop at the mandir. In India, there are mandirs in every town and village, and people call in for some quiet time before going back to their jobs for the day.

The most important and holy part of a mandir is the place where the statues of gods (murtis) are kept. This is called the **garbha-griha**. It is in the inner shrine or **vimana**, in the middle of the building. Over the garbha-griha is the tallest part of the mandir, which might be a tower, or a spire, or a dome. Many Hindus show respect for the murtis by walking around them.

When Hindus visit the mandir, they take off their shoes, to show respect and to keep the temple clean. Most mandirs have a porch or hall to keep the shoes. When Hindus go into the mandir, they pass small shrines which have statues of other gods connected with the ones in the garbha-griha. For example, if Rama is the main god of the mandir, Hanuman, the monkey god, might be in the small shrine, because Hanuman is connected with Rama.

The space in front of the garbha-griha is called the **mandapa**. This is where Hindus can gather to look at the murtis and make their offerings. Most Hindu mandirs have at least one priest, who takes the offerings from the worshippers and presents them to the murtis.

Discussion

Why do you think worship in the home is usually seen as the job of the woman?

Activity

1 Write a sentence about each of the following features of a mandir: the murtis; the garbha-griha; the vimana; the mandapa.

2 Describe what Hindus do when they worship at a shrine in the home. In your writing, say something about: washing before prayer; caring for the murtis; making offerings; prayer; arti.

Glossary words

deity

murti

puja

Gayatri mantra

arti

bhakti

mandir

garbha-griha

vimana

mandapa

Worship in the mandir

Worship in the mandir usually has three main features:

- **Bhajan** – the singing of holy songs, using words from famous Hindu poets.
- **Havan** – giving sacred fire to the gods. Fire stands for the god Agni. It is also used to make sacrifices, so using flames in worship is a very old way for Hindus to show a meeting with God. The priest uses butter and wood to light a small fire in front of the murtis (statues of the gods).
- **Arti** – the five flames of the arti lamp are waved in front of the murti. Then they are shared around the people, who pass their hands over the flame and then over their heads just as they do when worshipping at home.

Food and fasting

Most Hindus do not eat meat, because they believe in **ahimsa**, which means 'doing no harm'. They also think that eating meat stops people from being pure. Hindus believe that it is wrong to take life, because life comes from God. In India, meat costs more money than vegetables, and it is more difficult to keep fresh when the weather is hot.

Some Hindus eat meat, but they never eat beef, because the cow is holy in Hinduism. The bull is linked with the god Shiva, and the cow is linked with the god Krishna. The cow gives milk, and works in the fields pulling ploughs and carts, and cow manure is used to make fires. The cow is seen as a symbol of life. Cows are treated with great respect, and Hindus would never harm a cow or eat beef. It would result in bad karma, or bad luck.

Fasting is important for many Hindus. Going without food on holy days is seen as a good way of helping people to think about God. Only people who are fit and healthy go without all food. More often, Hindus only eat certain sorts of food and

go without others. Some people, mainly women, fast for one day each week.

The use of music and art in Hindu worship

Music is used for holy songs (bhajan) in worship. Sometimes people play drums or small finger cymbals. Dance is a popular way of telling stories of the gods, and it brings the stories to life, especially for children or people who cannot read. The costumes and hand and eye movements of Hindu dancers are part of a tradition which goes back for hundreds of years.

Art has always been an important part of Hinduism. Every Hindu home and temple has statues or pictures of the gods. In India, many of the mandirs are covered with carvings. Murtis (statues of the gods) are beautifully made from many materials. They give Hindus an object on which to focus their prayers and worship.

Sometimes, Hindu art is used for special occasions. At weddings, the hands and feet of the bride are painted with henna to make patterns known as **mehndi**. At the festival of Divali, patterns called *rangoli* are drawn.

Symbols in Hinduism

The most important symbol in Hinduism is the sacred sound **AUM**, sometimes spelt **Om**. It is found everywhere in Hinduism, in the temples and

in shrines in the home, and at weddings and on greetings cards. It is made of three sounds, A, U and M. It can mean:

- the three great gods, Brahma, Shiva and Vishnu
- the three worlds of earth, atmosphere, and heaven
- the cycle of birth, death and eternity
- three of the most important Hindu writings.

The **swastika** is also an important Hindu symbol. The swastika is very old, and means good fortune. It is used by Hindus at times of celebration, such as weddings and Divali.

Discussion

Do you think eating meat is a form of violence? Are there some animals you would eat, and others that you would not? Give reasons for your answers.

Activity

1 Why do many Hindus choose not to eat meat? (Try to use the word *ahimsa* in your answer.)

2 Explain why the cow is important for Hindus.

3 Draw the AUM symbol and the swastika, and write a sentence about each of them.

Glossary words

bhajan

havan

ahimsa

mehndi

AUM/Om

swastika

Islam

Muslim worship

'Islam' means submission to the will of Allah, and by doing this Muslims show what they believe.

The Five Pillars are at the centre of a Muslim's life:

● **Shahadah** – the statement of faith:

> There is no god except Allah, Muhammad ﷺ is the Messenger of Allah.

● **Salah** – praying five times a day so that Muslims can talk to Allah and worship him. The Prophet Muhammad ﷺ taught Muslims how they should pray. The prayers are said at fixed times and can be performed alone or with other people. The five set times are:

Fajr – from dawn until just before sunset

Zuhr – after midday until afternoon

'Asr – from late afternoon until just before sunset

Maghrib – after sunset until daylight ends

'Isha' – night until midnight or dawn

Before they pray Muslims must perform **wudu**. They wash their hands, mouth, nose, face, arms, head, ears and feet. Now they are ready to repeat the set prayers.

● **Zakah** – this is paying money to those in need. The money is used to help poorer Muslims and the community. Muslims pay 2½ % of their savings each year as zakah. Zakah began in the city of al-Madinah, to help widows and orphans. Muslims believe that wealth is a gift from Allah and should be shared. By giving zakah, the rest of a person's money is kept pure and people are not greedy or selfish. Muslims also make additional voluntary payments called **sadaqah**.

When praying, all Muslims follow a set of prayers and prayer positions as taught by Muhammad ﷺ.

- **Hajj** – the annual pilgrimage to Makkah, which each Muslim must carry out at least once in a lifetime if they can. A Muslim man who has completed Hajj is called Hajji, and a woman, Hajjah. The pilgrimage is made during Dhul Hijjah, the twelfth month.
- **Sawm** – fasting from just before dawn until sunset during the month of **Ramadan**, the ninth month. During daylight Muslims must not have any food or drink (including water), they must not smoke and they must not have sexual relations.

These are the five duties of every Muslim, which show obedience to God's wishes.

The Five Pillars are **ibadah** – acts of worship – which are carried out to obey Allah.

Shari'ah

Shari'ah means living your life according to Muslim law. In countries where the government is Muslim, the legal system is based on Shari'ah. Shari'ah itself is based on the teachings and instruction found in the Qur'an and Sunnah.

Arabic

Muslims worship in Arabic. This was the language of Muhammad ﷺ and the Qur'an is written in Arabic. All prayers are in Arabic and Muslims have a duty to learn Arabic so that they can understand, worship and also read the Qur'an.

Discussion

Do you think it is a good thing or a bad thing for a religion to have strict rules to follow?

Activity

Write a sentence about each of the Five Pillars.

Glossary words

Shahadah

Salah

wudu

zakah

sadaqah

Hajj

Sawm

Ramadan

ibadah

Shari'ah

The mosque

The mosque is the central place of worship for Muslims. Muslim men go there for **Salat-ul-Jumu'ah**, midday prayer on Fridays, and listen to the **khutbah** or speech given by the Imam.

The whole world can be thought of as a mosque because it is all created by God. Mosques belong to Allah and cannot be owned by any person or organisation. A mosque cannot be sold, mortgaged or rented.

Features of mosques

Many mosques are very beautiful buildings. The designs vary but there are certain features that all mosques must have.

The main open space in the mosque is the prayer hall. One wall faces the **Ka'bah** in **Makkah**, and a **mihrab** or niche in the wall shows Muslims the direction they must face when they pray. There is also a platform or **minbar** on which the Imam stands to give the khutbah. There will be a separate area for women to pray. This is behind a curtain or screen so that they will not distract the men.

Inside a mosque during prayer time.

Most mosques have at least one tower or **minaret** from which the **Adhan** or call to prayer is made. The dome represents the heavens and God's creation. There will also be running water so that people can perform wudu.

Mosques are usually very simple buildings and yet they may be highly decorated. There are no pictures, statues or photographs showing living beings because this would be against Muslim teaching. The walls are often decorated with verses from the Qur'an, the name and attributes of Allah and the name of Muhammad ﷺ written in Arabic.

The dome represents the heavens and God's creation.

Worship outside the mosque

The mosque is the centre of the Muslim community but most daily worship takes place in the home, where people pray and study the Qur'an. Because Muslims have to pray five times a day, they often have to do this at work or while they are travelling. The most important thing is that people pray. It does not matter where, but the place must be clean and the Muslim must face Makkah.

Music

Music is not used in Muslim worship. The Qur'an says:

> But there are, among men, those who purchase idle tales, without knowledge

(or meaning), to mislead (men) from the Path of Allah and throw ridicule (on the Path): for such there will be a humiliating penalty.

(Surah 31:6)

Music is seen as one of these 'idle' things that mislead people from the Path of Allah. The Prophet Muhammad ﷺ warned that:

> there will be (at some future time) people from my Ummah (nation) who will seek to make lawful... the use of musical instruments.
>
> (Sahih Al-Bukhari)

Tawhid and shirk

Tawhid and **shirk** are two very important ideas in Muslim belief.

Tawhid is the belief that there is only one God – Allah. This was a very important part of Muhammad's ﷺ message. Allah created and looks after the universe and he rules and controls everything that happens.

Muslims put Allah first in their lives. If they lived just to make money, this would be shirk. Shirk is a sin when people believe in anything except Allah or believe that something is as important as Allah.

Because of this, all images, pictures and statues are forbidden in Islam. Only Allah is the creator, and people should not try to create images of people or creatures.

Food and fasting

For the whole of the month of Ramadan, all adult Muslims must fast during the hours of daylight. Daylight is when someone can tell the difference between a white thread and a black thread.

> Until the white thread of dawn appear to you distinct from its black thread
>
> (Surah 2:187)

During the fast Muslims should not eat, drink, smoke or have any sexual activity. People can clean their teeth, though, and swallowing something by accident does not count.

If someone breaks their fast without a good reason they have to provide a meal for 60 people, or fast for another 60 days. Children, women during menstruation, pregnancy or breastfeeding, the old, the sick, travellers and soldiers do not have to fast. However, everyone except for children and old people should make up the missing days as soon as they can. Allah sees everything and knows what everyone is thinking, so there is no point in trying to cheat.

At the end of each day Muslims say:

> 'O God! For your sake we have fasted and now we break the fast with food you have given us.'

Each day, Muhammad ﷺ broke his fast with some dates or a drink, and most Muslims do the same. Later the whole family joins together for a big meal.

Discussion

Do you think music would help people in worship, or distract them?

Activity

1 Do you think it would be a good idea for everyone to have a regular fast like Ramadan?

2 What does *shirk* mean?

Glossary words

Salat-ul-Jumu'ah	minbar
khutbah	minaret
Ka'bah	Adhan
Makkah	tawhid
mihrab	shirk

Judaism

Jewish worship

Everyone who has a Jewish mother is a Jew and should follow the will of G-d. The Ten Commandments say how G-d wants people to live – this is also found in the **Shema**:

> Hear, O Israel: HASHEM is our G-d, HASHEM, the One and Only. You shall love HASHEM, your G-d, with all your heart, with all your soul and with all your resources. Let these matters that I command you today be upon your heart. Teach them thoroughly to your children and speak of them while you sit in your home, while you walk on the way, when you retire and when you arise. Bind them as a sign upon your arm and let them be tefillin between your eyes. And write them on the doorposts of your house and upon your gates.

This is the first of the three parts of the Shema. These can be found in the Torah in Deuteronomy 6:5–9, Deuteronomy 11:13–21 and Numbers 15:37–41.

Jews believe that G-d is everywhere, all powerful and all-knowing.

Jews believe they should show their love for G-d as they follow the 613 mitzvot (or commandments) which are found in the Torah. These give rules for life, including clothing, food, sexual relations, and prayer and worship.

The Temple

Many Jewish ceremonies are held in the home and with the family, but originally the centre of Jewish life and worship in Israel was the Temple in Jerusalem. This temple was first built by King Solomon and then rebuilt by Herod the Great.

People offered daily sacrifices here according to the rules in the Torah. At first, the Ark of the Covenant and the tablets of stone on which Moses had written the Ten Commandments were kept here.

Many attempts were made by other nations to take the Temple. It was destroyed by the armies of the Roman Empire in 70 CE and was never rebuilt. As the House of G-d it had provided a centre for Jews for prayer and worship. Jewish worship now takes place in the home and in the synagogues that are found in each Jewish community all over the world.

Jews should pray at least three times a day. These prayer times are:

Shacharit – dawn
Minchah – afternoon
Maariv – evening

Worship in the synagogue

Jews go to the synagogue to pray and to hear readings of the Torah. Services are held every day, but the most important time is **Shabbat**, when services are held on Friday evenings and on Saturday mornings.

Features of synagogues

Judaism is an ancient religion. After the destruction of the Temple, Jews moved to live all over the world. This spread of people is known as the **diaspora**. Jewish spiritual life and worship now have many different forms. Many synagogues are modern, with modern designs.

The synagogue is usually a plain building. The main room, or sanctuary, is an area of seats. The aron hakodesh, the ark which contains the Torah scrolls, is placed on the wall of the synagogue that faces towards Jerusalem. The scrolls are covered by a door or a curtain and have richly decorated covers as well as bells and a breastplate which represents the breastplate worn by the High Priest in the Temple.

Inside a synagogue

Some synagogues have a gallery for the women. This is to prevent the men being distracted from their prayers. In some other synagogues men and women are allowed to sit together.

Worship is led by a **chazan** who sings most of the service. In some Jewish services the singing is always unaccompanied on Shabbat. This is because playing musical instruments is seen as work and no form of work is permitted on Shabbat. In other synagogues an organ may be played.

Hebrew

Hebrew is the language of the Jews and the Torah is always read in Hebrew. In some synagogues the prayers during the service are in English, but in other synagogues all services and prayers are in Hebrew.

Jews believe that the Torah is the word of G-d and that it should be read in the original language. However, the scriptures are available in many languages for people to study, so that those who cannot read Hebrew can still understand them.

Discussion

Do you think music would help people in worship, or distract them?

Activity

Write a brief description of a synagogue, mentioning as many features as you can.

Glossary words

Shema

Shabbat

diaspora

menorah

bimah

chazan

There are no statues, pictures or photographs in the sanctuary because of the commandment that people should not make images of G-d's creation.

> You shall not make yourself a carved image nor any likeness of that which is in the heavens above or on the earth below or in the waters beneath the earth. You shall not prostrate yourself to them nor worship them; for I am HASHEM, your G-d – a jealous G-d.
>
> (Exodus 20:4–5)

There may be a seven-branched candlestick called a **menorah** which represents the candlestick that was in the Temple. There will also be a **bimah** or platform from which the Torah is read.

Worship in the home

The main place for worship for Jews is in the home with the family. Here Jews follow the food laws. On Friday evenings a special meal is prepared and two candles are lit to welcome Shabbat into the house. At the end of Shabbat the service of **havdalah** takes place as the new week begins. This worship reminds people of the importance of the family in Jewish life.

A man observing havdalah

In every Jewish home there are objects such as Shabbat candlesticks; a special plate and knife for the **challah** and a cloth to cover it; a havdalah spice box; a seder plate (for Pesach); and a **hanukiah**, the seven-branched candlestick used at **Hanukkah**. Also, on every doorpost (except the bathroom) there is a **mezuzah**.

Prayer

Prayer is a very important part of Judaism. If Jews are at home or at work during the prayer times, they will stop what they are doing and pray. There are set prayers for the times of day, including the Shema which is always said on getting up and on going to bed. Jews are also encouraged to pray in their own words.

Synagogue services consist almost entirely of readings from the Torah and Haftarah, and prayers taken from the Tenakh. Throughout the service people praise G-d.

Food and fasting

Judaism has religious laws about food and fasting. The food laws are very important in Jewish life and worship. In Genesis, G-d said that humans were rulers of all the animals (Genesis 1:26). G-d said that humans could eat seeds and fruits from plants (herbage):

> G-d said, 'Behold, I have given all herbage yielding seed that is on the surface of the entire earth, and every tree that has seed-yielding fruit; it shall be yours for food'.
>
> (Genesis 1:29)

At this point it seems that people were not meant to eat animals, but, after the flood, G-d told Noah:

> Every moving thing that lives shall be food for you; like the green herbage I have given you everything. But flesh; with its soul its blood you shall not eat.
>
> (Genesis 9:3–4)

This means that G-d told people they could eat all kinds of meat, provided that there was no blood in it.

When the Israelites were in the desert after they had escaped from Egypt, they were given more rules to follow. These can be found in the book of Leviticus (Leviticus 11:1–10, 13–23, 41–42).

> These are the creatures that you may eat from among all the animals that are upon the earth. Everything among the animals that has a split hoof, which is completely separated into double hooves, and that brings up its cud – that one you may eat...
>
> This may you eat from everything that is in the water: everything that has fins and scales in the water, in the seas, and in the streams, those may you eat.

There is also a list of birds as well as insects and reptiles, which Jews cannot eat.

As well as these rules, Jews are not allowed to eat the sciatic nerve of an animal:

> Therefore the Children of Israel are not to eat the displaced sinew on the hip-socket to this day, because he struck Jacob's hip-socket on the displaced sinew.
>
> (Genesis 32:32)

They are not allowed to mix dairy products and meat in the same meal:

> You shall not cook a kid in its mother's milk.
>
> (Deuteronomy 14:21b)

And, finally, they should not eat meat and fish together (Shulchan Arukh: Yoreh Deah 87:3).

The food that Jews can eat is called **kosher**. Kosher means 'permitted'. Food that Jews cannot eat is **terefah**. Terefah means 'forbidden'. All meat has to be slaughtered by **schechitah**: a blessing is said over the animal and it is killed by a single cut across the throat with a sharp knife. It is then hung upside down for the blood to drain out.

A shop selling kosher food

The food laws are central to Jewish life and are a very important part of Jewish worship.

Fasting

There are several days in the year when Jews fast but the most important is **Yom Kippur**. Yom Kippur is the Day of Atonement. Every year, in preparation for

Yom Kippur, Jews apologise to everyone whom they might have upset or hurt during the year. They also apologise to G-d for everything they have done wrong during the year.

On Yom Kippur, Jews fast for 25 hours to show they are obeying G-d's instructions. Fasting also helps Jews to concentrate on praying.

Discussion

Do you think it is easier to worship in a very plain building, or in one that is highly decorated?

Activity

Make a list of the foods which Jews cannot eat. Explain why each one is forbidden.

Gossary

havdalah

challah

hanukiah

Hanukkah

mezuzah

kosher

terefah

schechitah

Yom Kippur

Practice GCSE questions

Christianity

(a) Describe Christian attitudes towards the use of music and art in worship. (8 marks)

(b) Explain how the architecture of a church helps Christians to worship. (7 marks)

(c) 'God can be worshipped anywhere, so there is no need for churches.'
Do you agree? Give reasons to support your answer, and show that you have thought about different points of view. You must refer to Christianity in your answer. (5 marks)

Hinduism

(a) Describe Hindu attitudes towards the use of music and art in worship. (8 marks)

(b) Explain how the architecture of a mandir helps Hindus to worship. (7 marks)

(c) 'God can be worshipped anywhere, so there is no need for mandirs.'
Do you agree? Give reasons to support your answer, and show that you have thought about different points of view. You must refer to Hinduism in your answer. (5 marks)

Islam

(a) Describe Muslim attitudes towards the use of music and art in worship. (8 marks)

(b) Explain how the architecture of a mosque helps Muslims to worship. (7 marks)

(c) 'God can be worshipped anywhere, so there is no need for mosques.'
Do you agree? Give reasons to support your answer, and show that you have thought about different points of view. You must refer to Islam in your answer. (5 marks)

Judaism

(a) Describe Jewish attitudes towards the use of music and art in worship. (8 marks)

(b) Explain how the architecture of a synagogue helps Jews to worship. (7 marks)

(c) 'G-d can be worshipped anywhere, so there is no need for synagogues.'
Do you agree? Give reasons to support your answer, and show that you have thought about different points of view. You must refer to Judaism in your answer. (5 marks)

Tips

For all four questions

In part **(a)**, you are asked to describe religious attitudes to the use of art and music in worship. The religion you are studying might use music and art a lot. You might be able to give some examples of how and when they are used. Perhaps you have been studying a religion which does not agree with using music or art in worship. If so, you need to explain the reasons.

In part **(b)**, you need to be able to describe the architecture of the place of worship for the religion you have been studying. You should not draw in the exam. You need to use sentences to describe the building. A good answer would explain the different features. Think about the things a visitor might notice in the building. Say what they are and how they are used.

For part **(c)**, you are being tested to see how well you can understand different points of view. Think about how a religious believer would answer the question. Explain the reasons that they might give. Explain your own view. Imagine someone disagreeing, and explain what they might say and the reasons that they might give to support their opinion. They might think that religious buildings are a waste of money which should be given to the poor. They might think that religious buildings help people to think about God.

UNIT 3

Religion and Science

Introduction

Scientific theories about the origins of the world

Scientists know a lot more about the world than they did when many holy books were written. But have scientists shown that religion is wrong about how the world began?

In the past

People once thought that the earth was the centre of the universe. They thought the sun, moon and stars were nothing more than lights in the sky. They believed that the world is here just so that people can live in it.

Today

Now we know that our world is only one tiny planet. We know that there are many other life forms as well as our own.

Can people still believe that there is something special about human life?

The origins of the universe

Study of the way the universe began is called **cosmology**. Scientists believe that the universe is much older than people first imagined – about 18 billion years old. Some people even say there was never a 'beginning' at all, and the universe has always been here.

Most scientists believe that the universe was made by a **Big Bang**, which sent matter and gases flying out in all directions. As the gases cooled, they formed the stars and the planets, including the earth. There is evidence for this idea, which can be found with powerful telescopes.

The origins of humanity

Scientists often explain how people began, by using the theory of **evolution**. This theory was made famous by a man named Charles Darwin in the nineteenth century. He travelled the world on a ship called *The Beagle* to study animals and plants. Darwin believed that the animals and plants in the world today have developed slowly over millions of years.

Our planet is just one among many millions, and does not seem to be the centre of the universe at all.

When conditions change, such as the climate becoming warmer or colder, the strongest animals and plants survive and reproduce and the weaker ones die out (become extinct). This is known as **natural selection**. The next animals and plants are more like the stronger ones, and less like the weaker ones – they change, or **evolve**, to suit the new conditions. Darwin wrote his ideas in a book called *On the Origin of Species*.

Darwin's ideas meant that human beings must have evolved too. Long ago, humans did not exist as we know them today. People share some of their ancestors with apes. Humans are not very different from other animals. There must have been a time when there were no people at all, so perhaps the world was not made just for us. Perhaps the religious stories are not right.

Many people were shocked by Darwin's ideas at first. They could not believe they shared ancestors with apes. Newspaper cartoons made fun of Darwin. But when people started to find fossils which supported Darwin's ideas, people began to take him more seriously.

When Darwin first introduced his theory of evolution, people refused to believe it and made fun of him.

Does everything happen by chance?

Religious believers often say that the universe is here for a reason. They say that we are here as part of a big plan. But science often seems to say the opposite. It seems to say that we are here just by chance. There is no reason and no plan.

Science and religion in conflict

Some people think that science and religion can never agree. Perhaps people have to choose between science and religion. Perhaps one day scientists will come up with enough evidence to show that religion is all wrong. Possibly religious believers will one day be proved right, and will show that there is a God after all. But there are many people who have both a religious faith and a career in science. They think that the more we find out about the world, the more we can learn about God. Maybe it is possible to combine the two different ways of thinking, and to see science and religion as working together.

Discussion

Do we still need religious ideas to help us understand the universe, now that scientists have explained so much? You might think that we know much more now, and can do without ideas about God. Or you might think that science helps us to know more about God. You might think that God helps us to understand things that science can never explain.

Glossary words

cosmology

Big Bang

evolution/evolve

natural selection

# Christianity

Christian ideas about the origins of the world and of humanity

The Bible tells a story about how the world was made. It is not the same as the way scientists explain it. The book of Genesis teaches that the universe was made by God, and that God made it all out of nothing.

> In the beginning when God created the heavens and the earth, the earth was a formless void and darkness covered the face of the deep, while a wind from God swept over the face of the waters. Then God said, 'Let there be light', and there was light.
>
> (Genesis 1:1)

Genesis describes, in two stories, how God made the world for people to live in. God planned it all, and then put everything in its place.

Genesis says that all the animals and plants were made in the beginning:

> And God said, 'Let the earth bring forth living creatures of every kind: cattle and creeping things and wild animals of the earth of every kind.' And it was so. God made the wild animals of the earth of every kind, and the cattle of every kind, and everything that creeps upon the ground of every kind. And God saw that it was good.
>
> (Genesis 1:24–25)

The story suggests that when the animals were made, they looked just the same as they do today. It says nothing about creatures such as dinosaurs. Genesis says that all the animals were created at once. It does not say anything about evolution. It also says that people were present right from the beginning of the world.

In Genesis, when God made men and women they were the most important part of creation. They were made in the image of God, and given the Garden of Eden in which to live. Everything was perfect until Adam and Eve disobeyed God.

God made all the different animals. God showed them to the first man so that he could choose names for them:

> So out of the ground the Lord God formed every animal of the field and every bird of the air, and brought them to the man to see what he would call them; and whatever the man called every living creature, that was its name.
>
> (Genesis 2:19)

Some Christians find this teaching difficult because it is different from the views of science:
- It says the different species were there from the start and did not evolve.
- It does not say anything about a Big Bang.
- It suggests that the universe is about six thousand years old, but scientists say it is billions of years old.

Many modern Christians believe that the scientists are probably right, and that the universe began with a Big Bang. They also believe that people evolved gradually, and did not appear in the world as humans at the beginning of time. These Christians believe that the creation stories in the Bible are myths. They are stories which contain important truth, but are not to be taken literally. They say it shows how wonderful God really is; he does not just make life, but makes life that can evolve.

Some Christians, however, believe that the biblical accounts are literally true. The Bible, they believe, comes from God, and God does not make mistakes. People who believe that the biblical story of creation is literally true, are known as **creationists**.

The book of Genesis teaches that people were present on the Earth right from the beginning.

Christian views about people and animals

Christians believe people are different from other animals, because people have souls. In Genesis, when God makes Adam, he is special. People are made 'in the image of God':

> So God created humankind in his image, in the image of God he created them, male and female he created them.
>
> (Genesis 1:27)

It is not clear what it means to be made 'in the image of God'. Perhaps it means that the writers of Genesis thought that people actually looked like God. Perhaps they meant that humans share something of the nature of God.

> The Lord God formed man from the dust of the ground, and breathed into his nostrils the breath of life; and the man became a living being.
>
> (Genesis 2:7)

Christians believe that people have a soul. The soul is something that does not die when the body dies, but can live on after death. Human lives are sacred, and people have special rights and duties which other animals do not share.

Discussion

Do you think all Christians should believe that Genesis is literally true?

Do you think science shows that people do not need religion any more?

Activity

1 What do you think people might mean when they say that Genesis is a *myth*?

2 What is a *creationist*?

3 Explain why Christians might disagree about the theory of evolution. What is your own view?

Glossary words

creationist

Christian ideas about stewardship

Christians believe that people were put on the earth to act as 'stewards'. A steward is someone who looks after others, and is responsible for them. For example, at a festival a steward might show people where to park their cars or where to find lost children. In the Bible, people were told to be stewards of the world:

> Then God said, 'Let us make humankind in our image, according to our likeness; and let them have dominion over the fish of the sea, and over the birds of the air, and over the cattle, and over all the wild animals of the earth, and over every creeping thing that creeps upon the earth.
>
> (Genesis 1:26)

Christians believe that this means they are responsible for the world. They should care for it and protect it for the future. They should understand that the world belongs to God, and that it does not belong to them. The writer of Psalm 24 reminds people that God made the world:

> The earth is the Lord's, and all that is in it,
> The world, and those who live in it.
>
> (Psalm 24:1)

Greed

Christianity also teaches that people should not be greedy. They should think about God and about caring for the poor. Jesus taught that some things were more important than buying lots of things:

> He said to his disciples, 'Therefore I tell you, do not worry about your life, what you will eat, or about your body, what you will wear. For life is more than food, and the body more than clothing.'
>
> (Luke 12:22–23)

Although the Bible contains many teachings warning people about greed, people in rich countries still use far more

than they really need. They are using up the world's natural resources a lot more quickly than they can be replaced.

Christian responses to environmental issues

Christians have not always been concerned about environmental issues. Some people say Christians are to blame for making people think they have the right to do what they want with the world. The organisations that have done the most to help protect the environment have not been Christian.

Christianity teaches that people are responsible for the world. They are allowed to rule over the animals, but they should also protect them.

But today, Christians are much more aware that the environment faces problems. Many rainforests have been destroyed, too many fish have been taken from the sea, and people have dumped poisonous waste. Many animals and plants have been lost forever.

Most Christians believe that they have a duty to take better care of the world around them, because God told them to be stewards. Sometimes they join protests, such as those organised by Greenpeace or the Worldwide Fund for Nature.

Christians can also take more care to avoid harming the environment. For example, they might recycle things rather than just throw them away. They might try to limit car fumes by cycling to work or by using public transport. They might try to use their votes in ways that support care for the environment.

Discussion

Some people say that Christians are to blame for problems with the environment, because humans are supposed to rule over other animals and plants. Do you think this view is fair?

Activity

1 (a) Explain what a *steward* does.

  (b) Why do Christians believe that people are the *stewards* of the earth?

2 Find out more about the problems facing the environment today. You might visit the websites of Friends of the Earth or Greenpeace. Make a list of some of the ways in which Christians could help to conserve the environment.

Hinduism

Hindu ideas about the beginnings of the world

Hinduism teaches that no-one knows how the universe began. In a hymn called the Nasadiya Sukta, the writer asks how the world began from nothing:

> There was neither non-existence nor existence then; there was neither the realm of space nor the sky which is beyond.
>
> What stirred? Where? In whose protection? Was there water, bottomlessly deep?
>
> (Nasadiya Sukta)

This hymn shows feelings of awe and wonder. It does not say what might have happened. But other passages in Hindu writing give other ideas.

In a hymn known as the Purusha Sukta, the creation of the world is explained in a myth. A great 'cosmic man' is sacrificed in order to make the world. It is the first sacrifice, and it sets the pattern for Hindus to make sacrifices to the gods every day in their homes as well as in the temples. When sacrifices are made, the gods keep the world going. In the Purusha Sukta, different parts of the 'cosmic man', known as Purusha, make different parts of the universe:

> His mouth became the Brahmin; his arms were made into the Warrior, his thighs the People, and from his feet the Servants were born. The moon was born from his mind; from his eye the sun was born. Indra and Agni came from his mouth, and from his vital breath the Wind was born.
>
> (Purusha Sukta 12, 13)

This hymn teaches that the different social classes, or **varnas**, were formed from the beginning of the world. In the hymn, animals and plants were all created separately in the beginning as well. There is nothing about evolution.

But Hindus also teach that the whole of nature works in a cycle. Everything changes all the time. Things come into being, grow, change, fade away and die, and then other things come into being again and the whole cycle repeats itself. The theory of evolution fits in quite well with this belief.

The Nasadiya Sukta does not give an answer to questions of how the world came into being. It says that it is a mystery that we will probably never understand.

The religious beliefs of Hindus do not clash with the theories of science in the way that many other beliefs do. This is because, in Hinduism, there is no absolute set of beliefs which everyone has to have. People have many different understandings of God, and are still Hindus. Because there are no rules about what must be believed, it is not a problem if Hindus agree with science about how the world began.

The Hindu writings give different ideas about the origins of the world. Some say that the world was made by God. Others say that the gods were made after the world was formed. Some say that the world has always existed, so there was no creation at all. The central message of Hindu teaching about the origins of the world is that it is a mystery.

Discussion

Do you think scientists will ever completely understand how the world began?

Activity

1 Explain what the Purusha Sukta teaches about the beginnings of the world.

2 Why do you think that religions often use myths to explain how the world began, instead of just giving facts?

Glossary words

varnas

Hindu views about people and animals

Hindus believe that all living things are related to one other, because they all come from God. Many Hindus believe that when people are reborn, they might come back as a person, but they might come back as an animal. So an animal might be your relation, from an earlier life. Perhaps, in past lives, a boy and his dog used to be brothers. Many Hindus are vegetarian because killing an animal for food might mean killing someone from your family. They also think meat is not clean.

Animals are linked with many of the Hindu gods. The animals are 'vehicles' (**vahana**) of the gods. For example, the peacock is the vehicle of the goddess Saraswati, and the tortoise is linked with the elephant-headed god Ganesha.

Peacocks are protected animals in India, because of their association with the goddess Saraswati.

Hindus believe that humans have no right to treat animals with cruelty. **Ahimsa** (harmlessness) is very important in Hinduism, and this includes not harming animals.

Hindu responses to environmental issues

In India, many people are very poor. Some issues to do with environment do not matter as much in India as they do in Britain. For example, the waste of wrapping and bags in supermarkets does not matter in India, where most of the food is grown at home or bought from the market, and when there is often not much to buy. Poor people always recycle things because they do not have the money to buy new ones. Very poor people sometimes search rubbish dumps, in the hope of finding something useful that someone else has thrown away. Many homes do not have cars or electricity, so most people do not waste fuel.

In India, it matters that people do not pollute water, because diseases such as cholera and typhoid spread quickly. People need to get rid of rubbish carefully, to keep rats and mice away.

For Hindus, there are two main reasons for wanting to protect the environment:

● The whole world is part of God. Caring for the world is a way of caring for God.
● Hindus believe they will be born again into this world after they die. So the future of the planet matters to them because they will be living in it when they are reborn.

Hindus in India care about environmental issues such as planting trees, to try and protect wildlife and to help save water. Some Hindus are interested in finding new ways of making electricity.

People in rich countries often make problems with the environment even worse. The rich countries make the oil which is sometimes spilt into the sea.

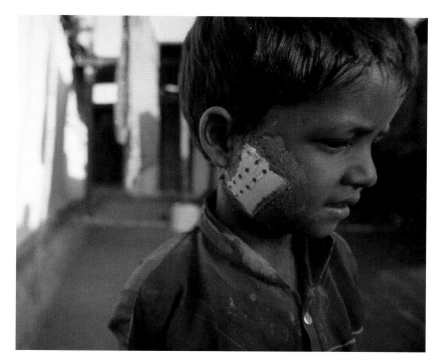

Thousands of Hindus died when poisonous gas leaked from a chemical factory in Bhopal. Many others were badly injured.

Rich countries use most of the world's food and fuel. But it is often poor people who suffer when there are problems with the environment. For example, if there is climate change, floods can destroy everything the poor people own. If the seas are polluted or over-fished, the poor fishermen are the first to suffer.

The worst chemical accident in world history happened in India. In 1984, a chemical factory in Bhopal leaked a deadly poisonous gas. Thousands of people were killed. Many more died slow and painful deaths over the next few years, or were blinded or suffered other serious injuries. This event led to the chemical industry producing much stricter rules about safety and the protection of the environment.

Discussion

Do you think that rich countries should do more for the environment than poor countries? Or do you think the same rules should apply to everyone?

Activity

1 Explain why Hindus usually show respect for animals.

2 (a) What are the main environmental issues for Hindus?

   (b) Car pollution and wasting electricity are not as important in India as in the UK. Why is this?

Glossary words

vahana

ahimsa

Islam

Muslim ideas about the origins of the world and of humanity

The Qur'an says that Allah created the world, and life:

> Your Guardian-Lord is Allah, Who created the heavens and the earth in six Days, then He established Himself on the Throne (of authority): He draweth the night as a veil o'er the day, each seeking the other in rapid succession: He created the sun, the moon, and the stars, (all) governed by laws under His Command...
>
> It is He Who sendeth the Winds like heralds of glad tidings, going before His Mercy: when they have carried the heavy-laden clouds, We drive them to a land that is dead, make rain to descend thereon, and produce every kind of harvest therewith...
>
> From the land that is clean and good, by the Will of its Cherisher, springs up Produce, (rich) after its kind...
>
> (Surah 7:53–58)

The Qur'an does not say what order things were created in, but it does say that Allah created everything. The word 'days' is an Arabic word *ayyam* which can mean 'long periods' or 'ages'. So the Qur'an is saying that Allah created the universe over a long period of time.

The creation of humans is also explained in the Qur'an, and Allah says that humans were created to serve Allah:

> I have created Jinns and men, that they may serve Me. No Sustenance do I require of them, nor do I require that they should feed Me. For Allah is He Who gives (all) Sustenance – Lord of Power – Steadfast (forever).
>
> (Surah 51:56–57)

The **Jinn** are spirits made of fire. They are neither good nor evil. Allah also made **mala'ikah**, who are angels and messengers of Allah. They have no bodies but they can take on human shape.

Islam and science

Islam has had a close link to science, and modern scientific ideas about the creation of the earth do not create any problems for Muslims. They believe that the Qur'an is the Word of Allah and true, but that science can help explain what is said in the Qur'an.

The Qur'an does have some details about the creation of the world that scientists today also talk about:

> Do not the unbelievers see that the heavens and earth were joined together (as one unit of Creation), before We clove them asunder? We made from water every living thing? Will they not then believe?... It is He Who created the Night and the Day, and the sun and the moon: all (the celestial bodies) swim along, each in its rounded course.
>
> (Surah 21:30, 33)

The Qur'an says here that Allah made every living thing from water. Scientists today think that life began in water. The Qur'an says that the planets (celestial bodies) move in a 'rounded course'. This is lke the scientific notion of orbits – planets going around the sun. The Qur'an also explains about water and its role in the growth of life:

> Seest thou not that Allah sends down rain from the sky, and leads it through springs in the earth? Then He causes to grow, therewith, produce of various colours: then it withers; thou wilt see it grow yellow; then He makes it dry up and crumble away.
>
> (Surah 39:21)

Because the Qur'an contains these explanations of life, scientific discoveries are welcomed because they help people understand what Allah created.

Discussion

'Scientific theories about the origins of life are bound to be more reliable than those in ancient sacred texts.' What do you think about this statement? Do other people have a different point of view from yours?

Activity

Write a short paragraph explaining what Muslims believe about the creation of the earth and the life on it.

Glossary words

Jinn

mala'ikah

Muslim ideas about the place of humanity in the world

Allah is seen as the creator of the world and humans are here to look after it but they do not own it. Their job is to look after the world for God and for future generations.

This passage says that people should not try to change things that Allah has created. People should work to look after things as Allah has created them:

> So set thou thy face steadily and truly to the Faith: (establish) Allah's handiwork according to the pattern on which He has made mankind: no change (let there be) in the work (wrought) by Allah.
>
> (Surah 30:30)

This Surah shows how people can be sure that Allah created everything and makes sure that all creation follows his design:

> Allah is He Who raised the heavens without any pillars that ye can see; then He established Himself on the Throne (of Authority); He has subjected the sun and the moon (to his Law)! Each one runs (its course) for a term appointed. He doth regulate all affairs, explaining the Signs in detail, that ye may believe with certainty in the meeting with your Lord. And it is He Who spread out the earth, and set thereon mountains standing firm, and (flowing) rivers: and fruit of every kind He made in pairs, two and two: He draweth the Night as a veil o'er the Day. Behold, verily in these things there are Signs for those who consider!
>
> (Surah 13:2–3)

This passage says that Allah cares for the world and everything in it. People are trusted by Allah to look after his creation:

> Say: 'Shall I seek for (my) Cherisher other than Allah, when He is the Cherisher of all things (that exist)?' Every soul draws the meed of its acts on none but itself: no bearer of burdens can bear the burden of another.

> Your goal in the end is towards Allah: He will tell you the truth of the things wherein ye disputed. It is He Who hath made you (His) agents, inheritors of the earth...
>
> (Surah 6:164–165)

Muslims are constantly giving thanks to Allah for his Creation and for their food:

> The Earth is green and beautiful, and Allah has appointed you his stewards over it.

> The whole earth has been created a place of worship, pure and clean.

> Whoever plants a tree and diligently looks after it until it matures and bears fruit is rewarded.

> If a Muslim plants a tree or sows a field and humans and beasts and birds eat from it, all of it is love on his part.
>
> (Hadith)

Animals

Islam believes that humanity has a responsibility to look after animals:

> And take not life – which Allah has made sacred – except for just cause.
>
> (Surah 17:33)

The Prophet said that animals must be treated well. He told a story of a prostitute who, on a hot day, took water from a well to give to a dog. For this act of kindness, he said, Allah forgave her all her sins.

Muslim responses to environmental issues

Many Muslim countries are dry and have large areas of desert. This has made it important to look after the places that have water – not to pollute water, since it is precious, and to care for the soil and plants as people depend on them.

At the World Wide Fund for Nature International at Assisi in 1986, the Muslim representative, Dr Abdullah Omar Nasseef, stressed the human responsibility to look after the earth:

How might the desert region where Islam began have shaped Muslim ideas about the environment?

The central concept of Islam is tawhid or the Unity of God. Allah is Unity; and His Unity is also reflected in the unity of mankind, and the unity of man and nature. His trustees are responsible for maintaining the unity of His creation, the integrity of the Earth, its flora and fauna, its wildlife and natural environment. Unity cannot be had by discord, by setting one need against another or letting one end predominate over another; it is maintained by balance and harmony. Therefore Muslims say that Islam is the middle path and we will be answerable for how we have walked this path, how we have maintained balance and harmony in the whole of creation around us.

So unity, trusteeship and accountability, that is tawhid, khalifa and akhrah, the three central concepts of Islam, are also the pillars of the environmental ethics of Islam. They constitute the basic values taught by the Qur'an. It is these values which led Muhammad ﷺ, the Prophet of Islam, to say: 'Whoever plants a tree and diligently looks after it until it matures and bears fruit is rewarded'.

Islam believes that God has created the world for us to live in and that every effort must be made to be 'green' and to protect the environment.

Discussion

What are the responsibilities of being given control over the earth?

Activity

1 Why do Muslims show respect for animals?

2 Why are Muslims concerned about the environment?

Judaism

Jewish ideas about the origins of the world and of humanity

The Jewish scriptures begin with G-d's creation of the world:

> In the beginning of G-d's creating the heavens and the earth – when the earth was astonishingly empty, with darkness upon the surface of the deep, and the Divine Presence hovered upon the surface of the waters – G-d said, 'Let there be light', and there was light. G-d saw that the light was good, and G-d separated between the light and the darkness. G-d called to the light: 'Day', and to the darkness He called: 'Night'. And there was evening, and there was morning, one day.
>
> (Genesis 1:1–5)

Jewish belief is that these books were written down by Moses but were revealed to him by G-d. This means that they are the 'Word of G-d'. If this is the case, then the stories in them should be true.

Sometimes there are difficulties in understanding the stories when something is repeated. One of these problems is in the account of the creation of human beings.

In the first chapter of Genesis it says:

> So G-d created Man in His image, in the image of G-d he created Him; male and female He created them.
>
> (Genesis 1:27)

But in the second chapter it says that G-d first created a man from dust and then created a woman out of the man:

> And HASHEM G-d formed the man of dust from the ground, and He blew into his nostrils the soul of life; and the man became a living being.
>
> So HASHEM G-d cast a deep sleep upon the man and he slept; and He took one of his sides and He filled in flesh in its place.

Then HASHEM G-d fashioned the side that He had taken from the man into a woman, and He brought her to the man. And the man said, 'This time it is bone of my bones and flesh of my flesh. This shall be called Woman, for from man was she taken.'

> (Genesis 2:7, 21–23)

Some people say that these are just two versions of the same thing. Others think that it shows there are two different people writing. The first story shows G-d creating man and woman at the same time and so they appear equal. In the second story man is created first and woman is just part of him. Some people say that this means women are less important than men.

Jews believe that the Torah is the Word of G-d

There are also problems with modern scientific explanations of creation and evolution. If the Torah story of the creation is true then people cannot accept the scientific versions. Other people say that the story is just an attempt to show how G-d looks after the world. It does not have to be literally true for this message to be understood.

Humans in creation

The passage below shows a Jewish belief about the place of humans in creation. The writer marvels at how G-d, who is all-powerful and has created an entire universe, should give humans so much, even though we are so weak:

> HASHEM, our Master, how mighty is Your Name throughout the earth, [You] Who places Your majesty on the heavens. Out of the mouths of babes and sucklings You have established strength, because of Your enemies, to silence foe and avenger. When I behold Your heavens, the work of Your fingers, the moon and the stars that You have set in place, [I think,] 'What is frail man that You should remember him, and the son of mortal man that You should be mindful of him?' Yet, You have made him but slightly less than the angels, and crowned him with soul and splendor. You give him dominion over Your handiwork, You placed everything under his feet: sheep and cattle, all of them, even the beasts of the field; the birds of the sky and the fish of the sea; for [man] even traverses the lanes of the sea. HASHEM, our Master, how mighty is Your Name throughout the earth!

(Psalm 8: 2–10)

This passage says that humans have a very important place in G-d's creation. Humans are in charge of the world ('dominion over Your handiwork'). Humans also have authority over all life on earth.

Discussion

What difference does it make whether the Torah is the word of G-d or writings by people who were inspired?

Activity

Write a paragraph explaining the problems of believing that the Torah was revealed by G-d.

Jewish ideas about the place of humanity in the world

The relationship between people and animals

In Jewish scriptures, animals are seen as very valuable and they were offered as sacrifices to G-d in the Temple in Jerusalem. In Genesis, G-d gave Adam control over all the animals:

> And G-d said, 'Let us make Man in our Own image, after Our likeness. They shall rule over the fish of the sea, the birds of the sky, and over the animals, the whole earth, and every creeping thing that creeps upon the earth.' So G-d created Man in His image, in the image of G-d He created him; male and female He created them. G-d blessed them and G-d said to them, 'Be fruitful and multiply, fill the earth and subdue it; and rule over the fish of the sea, the birds in the sky, and every living thing that moves on the earth.'
>
> (Genesis 1:26–28)

and:

> Now, HASHEM G-d had formed out of the ground every beast of the field and every bird of the sky, and brought them to the man to see what he would call each one; and whatever the man called each living creature, that remained its name. And the man assigned names to all the cattle and to the birds of the sky and to every beast of the field.
>
> (Genesis 2:19–20)

Knowing the name of a person or animal was believed to give you special power over them. This is the beginning of the idea of stewardship, that people have a responsibility to look after the world.

The Torah teaches that animals are to be shown respect. One teaching, from Proverbs 12:10, says that 'The righteous one knows [the needs of] his animal's soul'. This means that people who obey G-d's laws will treat animals properly, without cruelty. Another teaching says 'You shall not muzzle an ox in its threshing (Deuteronomy 25:4) – putting a muzzle on would be unpleasant for the ox.

A very important commandment for Jews is to keep the seventh day of the week, Shabbat, sacred to G-d. Religious Jews do no work on Shabbat.

Animals are also mentioned in the Ten Commandments – they are to be rested, on Shabbat also:

> Safeguard the Sabbath day to sanctify it, as HASHEM, your G-d, has commanded you. Six days shall you labour and accomplish all your work; but the seventh day is Sabbath to HASHEM, your G-d, you shall not do any work – you, your son, your daughter, your slave, your maidservant, your ox, your donkey, and your every animal, and your convert within your gates, in order that your slave and your maidservant may rest like you.
>
> (Deuteronomy 5:12–14)

There are no Jewish teachings on the use of animals for scientific experiments, but these experiments should be necessary and, as far as possible, suffering should be avoided.

Jewish responses to environmental issues

Every year, at the New Year festival of Rosh Hashanah, Jews thank G-d for the creation of the world, because:

> HASHEM's is the earth and its fullness, the inhabited land and those who dwell in it.
>
> (Psalm 24:1)

Jews show their respect for trees in the annual festival of Tu B'Shevat – New Year for Trees. This takes place on the 15th day of the Jewish month of Shevat. This has been especially important since the

In Israel, irrigation schemes have 'made the desert bloom'.

founding of the State of Israel in 1948. Israelis have worked to plant trees in the desert to turn it back into useful land.

There is a law in the Torah about trees:

> When you besiege a city for many days to wage war against it to seize it, do not destroy its trees by swinging an axe against them...
>
> (Deuteronomy 20:19a)

Another rule applies to the use of the land. The book of Leviticus says that once every 50 years the land should be rested in a Year of Jubilee so that it will give a better harvest in the future (Leviticus 25:8–11). Environmentalists agree that resting the land is very important. Over-production causes environmental problems like soil erosion and deforestation.

At the 1986 World Wide Fund for Nature international conference held at Assisi, Rabbi Arthur Hertzberg said:

> ...when the whole world is in peril, when the environment is in danger of being poisoned and various species, both plant and animal, are becoming extinct. It is our Jewish responsibility to put the defence of the whole of nature at the very centre of our concern... The encounter of G-d and man in nature is thus conceived in Judaism as a seamless web with man as the leader and custodian of the natural world. Even in the many centuries when Jews were most involved in their own immediate dangers

and destiny, this universalist concern has never withered. In this century, Jews have experienced the greatest tragedy of their history when one third of their people were murdered by unnatural men and, therefore, we are today particularly sensitive to the need for a world in which each of G-d's creations is what He intended it to be. Now, when the whole world is in peril, when the environment is in danger of being poisoned and various species, both plant and animal, are becoming extinct, it is our Jewish responsibility to put the defence of the whole of nature at the very centre of our concern. Two men were out on the water in a rowboat. Suddenly, one of them started to saw under his feet. He maintained that it was his right to do whatever he wished with the place which belonged to him. The other answered him that they were in the rowboat together; the hole that he was making would sink both of them.

> (Vayikra Rabbah 4:6)

In the Jewish prayer book there are blessings. They show how Jews see the work of G-d in everything around them:

> Blessed are You, HASHEM, our G-d, King of the universe,
> (on seeing the ocean)
> Who made the great sea
> (on seeing very beautiful people, trees or fields)
> Who has such in His universe
> (on smelling a fragrance)
> Who creates species of fragrance
> (on smelling fruit or nuts)
> Who places a good aroma into fruits

Discussion

How has Jewish concern for the environment helped to 'make the desert bloom' in Israel?

Activity

1 What is meant by *stewardship*?

2 How do Jews show their respect for trees?

Practice GCSE questions

Christianity

(a) Describe Christian beliefs about how the world began. (8 marks)

(b) Explain how and why a Christian might show concern for the environment. (7 marks)

(c) 'Scientific ideas about how the universe began prove that Christianity is wrong.'
Do you agree? Give reasons to support your answer and show that you have thought about different points of view. (5 marks)

Hinduism

(a) Describe Hindu beliefs about how the world began. (8 marks)

(b) Explain how and why a Hindu might show concern for the environment. (7 marks)

(c) 'Scientific ideas about how the universe began prove that Hinduism is wrong.'
Do you agree? Give reasons to support your answer and show that you have thought about different points of view. (5 marks)

Islam

(a) Describe Muslim beliefs about how the world began. (8 marks)

(b) Explain how and why a Muslim might show concern for the environment. (7 marks)

(c) 'Scientific ideas about how the universe began prove that Islam is wrong.'
Do you agree? Give reasons to support your answer and show that you have thought about different points of view. (5 marks)

Judaism

(a) Describe Jewish beliefs about how the world began. (8 marks)

(b) Explain how and why a Jew might show concern for the environment. (7 marks)

(c) 'Scientific ideas about how the universe began prove that Judaism is wrong.'
Do you agree? Give reasons to support your answer and show that you have thought about different points of view. (5 marks)

Tips

For all four questions

In part **(a)**, you need to be able to describe clearly the beliefs you have studied. You might be able to refer to some sacred texts to illustrate the points you make. Remember that not all people think alike, even if they belong to the same religion. You might be able to show why some religious believers are happy to accept the views of science. You could also say why other people disagree.

In part **(b)**, you need to think about how religion might affect someone's opinion about the environment. Why might they believe that it is important to care for the planet? How do their religious beliefs influence their opinions? You also need to say something about how they might put these ideas into practice. Perhaps there are organisations they might join, or ways in which they could care for the environment in their everyday lives.

In part **(c)**, you need to try and think about different points of view, and the reasons why people might have different opinions about science and religion. How might a member of the religion you have been studying feel about the views of science? Why might they think this way? You also need to explain your own view, and give your reasons.

UNIT 4
Death and the Afterlife

Christianity

Christian beliefs about the soul

Christians believe that a person is more than just a mind and body. They believe that each person also has a soul. The soul cannot be seen, it never dies, and it makes people different from every other kind of animal.

In the book of Genesis, people were made in God's image:

> So God created humankind in his image, in the image of God he created them; male and female he created them.
>
> (Genesis 1:27)

No-one is sure what it means to be made 'in the image of God'. But many Christians think it means that God put something of his own nature into each person, and this is called the 'soul'.

According to Genesis, when other animals were made they were just formed 'out of the ground' (Genesis 2:19), but when Adam was made, God gave him an extra kind of life:

> The Lord God formed man from the dust of the ground, and breathed into his nostrils the breath of life; and the man became a living being.
>
> (Genesis 2:7)

As Christian thought developed, Christians began to believe that people have souls, which are separate from the body and do not die when the body dies. The soul makes each person special. Christians believe that human life is very valuable to God, because humans have souls. They think animals do not have souls and this is why most Christians are happy to eat meat.

St Paul, who was one of the first Christians, taught that the body and the soul often want different things. The soul lives for ever, but the body dies. The soul wants to be with God, and to do what is right. But the body often wants other things, such as food and treats. Paul wrote:

> To set the mind on the flesh is death, but to set the mind on the Spirit is life and peace.
>
> (Romans 8:6)

Paul also taught that when people die, the 'spiritual body' or soul lives for ever. For Paul, the **resurrection** of Jesus was proof of life after death. Christians can expect that they will be raised back to life by the power of God, because of what happened to Jesus.

Understanding hell, heaven and purgatory

Hell

In the past, belief in heaven and hell was very important for Christians. But today Christians think more about life after death in heaven. They usually think of hell as a way of describing being without God, not as a real place.

Christians in the Middle Ages thought about hell a lot. They believed it was a place of torture for people who had turned their backs on Christianity and who had done wrong. They told others to join the church, by saying that they would go to hell if they refused. Today, some Christians believe that there is a hell where people will go if they are not Christians. But most Christians talk about a loving and forgiving God.

Heaven

Christians believe that when they die, the body is not needed any more, but the soul goes on to live for ever with God. This is known as 'heaven'. In Christian art and writing, heaven is often seen as a place with angels playing on harps, as a way of describing something that is very difficult to put into words.

The **Apostles' creed** is a Christian statement of belief. Many Christians say it at church. Part of it states the Christian hope of life after death:

> I believe in ... the forgiveness of sins
> The resurrection of the body
> And the life everlasting.

Christians believe that at the end of life, the soul is raised from the dead and lives on in a new way. Some Christians believe that one day, the world will come to its Last Days. Then people's bodies will come back to life. Because of this belief, they prefer to be buried rather than cremated. But most others think that there are problems with this idea, because if heaven is perfect, then people ought to be able to live with new, perfect bodies, and not need their old ones any more.

Beliefs about heaven are difficult to put into words, because it is nothing like the way that we live on the earth. Most Christians say that they cannot know what heaven will be like. But they do believe that it will last for ever with God. There will be no more evil and suffering.

Purgatory

In Roman Catholic teaching, purgatory is a state after death, for people who are not ready to go straight to heaven. Their souls stay in purgatory until they are free from sin. Roman Catholics often pray for the souls of those who have died, in the hope that they will not have to spend too long in purgatory.

Discussion

What are your own beliefs about life after death? Do you think people continue to exist in a new way in heaven or hell after they have died? Or do you believe that people are reborn back into this world? Or do they just stop? Or something else?

Activity

1 Explain what Christians mean by:

(a) *heaven*

(b) *hell*

(c) *purgatory*.

2 What do you think happens to people after they die? Try to give reasons to support your answer.

Glossary words

resurrection

Apostles' creed

In the Middle Ages Christians believed literally in heaven and hell. In this picture from 1306, the artist Giotto shows his understanding of what heaven and hell would be like.

God as judge

Christians believe that God knows people, and will judge what they do. They believe that God will look at how well they have cared for the poor and the weak. The Parable of the Sheep and the Goats, in Matthew's Gospel, teaches that a Day of Judgement will come when God will put people into two groups. The people who have cared about the poor will live for ever with God, but the people who have been selfish will be sent away from God into hell.

> Then he will say to those on his left, 'Depart from me, you who are cursed, into the eternal fire prepared for the devil and his angels.
>
> For I was hungry and you gave me nothing to eat, I was thirsty and you gave me nothing to drink,
>
> I was a stranger and you did not invite me in, I needed clothes and you did not clothe me, I was sick and in prison and you did not look after me.'
>
> They also will answer, 'Lord, when did we see you hungry or thirsty or a stranger or needing clothes or sick or in prison, and did not help you?'
>
> He will reply, 'I tell you the truth, whatever you did not do for one of the least of these, you did not do for me.'
>
> Then they will go away to eternal punishment, but the righteous to eternal life.
>
> (Matthew 25:41–46)

But Christianity also teaches that God is loving and forgiving. Christians believe that everyone has done wrong, but they will be forgiven if they are really sorry, because of their faith in Christ. When Paul wrote to the new churches in the early days of Christianity, he told them that they should not worry about being judged:

> There is therefore now no condemnation for those who are in Christ Jesus. For the law of the Spirit of life in Christ Jesus has set you free from the law of sin and of death.
>
> (Romans 8:1)

Christians believe that the death of Jesus gave people the chance to be forgiven, as long as they see the wrong they have done and make up their minds to be better in the future.

Christian funerals

Christians, like everyone else, are sad when someone they love dies. A Christian funeral service teaches that death is not the end. Christians share the hope that after death, they will live for ever with God. The Christian funeral service reminds them of this hope. A Christian funeral begins with the words of Jesus:

> I am the resurrection and the life.

In most Christian churches, at a funeral there is a short service. A passage of the Bible is read, about the hope of eternal life. Prayers are said asking God to comfort the family and friends, and giving thanks for the life of the person who has died. There might be a short talk about the person, to remember what he or she did, and sometimes a hymn is sung. A funeral service is always sad, but the person leading the service usually tries not to allow it to become too gloomy. The people remember the good things about the person's life. They try to be grateful to have known him or her.

After the service, the dead person might be buried in a coffin in the ground, or might be cremated. The minister will say more prayers, asking God to look after the dead person's soul. The people remember that all life is given by God and that God decides when to take it away.

Christians believe that although death is very sad, it is not the end.

After the funeral, the people at the service often go back to the house of the close family. They have something to eat and drink and there is a chance to talk.

Discussion

Do you think funerals are a good idea? Or do they make things harder for the family and friends? Would it be better just to have a funeral or cremation without any speeches, readings, hymns or prayers? Give reasons for your answer.

Activity

1 Explain the main features of a Christian funeral service.

2 Why do you think that Christian funerals remind people of life after death?

Hinduism

Atman

Hindus believe that in every person there is an eternal 'soul', known as **Atman**. Each person has a body, which is how we recognise each other. But the body changes and grows old; it can be hurt, and in the end it dies. The Atman is different. It lives on for ever. When one body is worn out and dies, the Atman is born again into a new life as a different person. Atman is perfect. It cannot be killed, and it does not get old like the body. It cannot become ill, or be hurt in any way.

Each Atman can be reborn in many different lives, over hundreds or thousands of years. A good person earns good **karma**, and a bad person earns bad karma. Then the karma has to be lived out as good or bad luck. The Atman will carry on being reborn over and over again. This process is known as **rebirth**, or **reincarnation**.

Rebirth

Sometimes, if people go to a new place, they feel as though they have been there before, even though they never have. Sometimes, people meet someone for the first time and yet think they know that person. There are also people such as Mozart who show great skills from a very young age. Mozart wrote music at an age when many children cannot even read. Hindus would say that when these things happen, they come from past lives. A few people develop great skill in meditation and they can sometimes bring back much clearer memories of past lives.

Samsara and rebirth

The Hindu word **samsara** refers to the way people are reborn over and over again. When the body dies, the Atman is born into a new body. It happens in a cycle, just like the water cycle or the nitrogen cycle in the natural world.

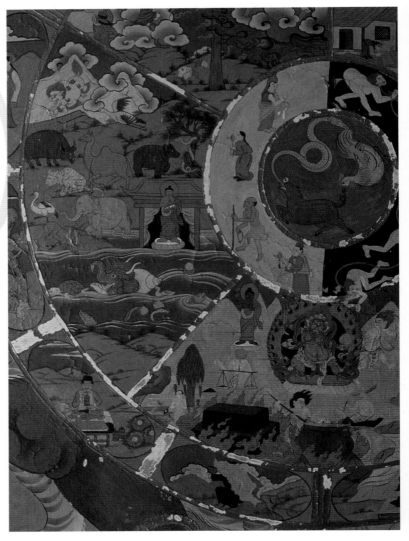

The cycle of birth and death goes on through many hundreds of lives.

Many people like the idea of living lots of times, even if they are not Hindu. It might be good to have a different job next time, or to be born in a different part of the world. But Hindus believe that samsara goes on and on, and that it would be good to escape from it. Hindus hope one day to reach **moksha**. Moksha is the name given to the freedom of Atman from the cycle of birth, death and rebirth, so that it no longer has to be born back into the world but can become a part of God. Hinduism teaches that there are different ways to achieve moksha. One of them is by loving God, and another is by trying to become wise.

Rebirth and moral behaviour

Hindus believe that the way people behave affects what will happen to them in the next life. Everything that a person does, in Hindu teaching, has 'fruits', and this is known as the *law of karma*. Good deeds will bring rewards for the person who does them. Bad actions such as stealing, unkindness or greed will bring punishments. This does not always happen in the same lifetime. We can see that there are some people who live good lives, but bad things happen to them. We also see that people who do wrong often get away with it. Hinduism teaches that the karma from one life is carried over into the next. Reward or punishment may happen in a future life.

Each person's fate depends on how well they have behaved. If they behave badly, then in their next life they might be born into a very poor family. They might be disabled, or live a very short life, or suffer in some way. So Hindus do what they can to build up good karma. They try to say all their prayers and be kind to others, so that they can have a good rebirth in the next life.

Some people say that Hindus will feel that other people's problems are their own fault. They disagree with the Hindu way of thinking, because it seems to be saying that if people are poor or disabled, it serves them right because of the way they have lived in the past.

Discussion

Have you ever felt anything which made you think you had lived before? Do you think that this is evidence of rebirth, or do you think that something else could explain it?

Activity

1 Explain what Hindus mean by:

   (a) *Atman*

   (b) *samsara*

   (c) *karma*

   (d) *moksha*.

2 Describe in your own words what a Hindu would say if they were asked about life after death.

Glossary words

Atman

karma

rebirth/reincarnation

samsara

moksha

Funeral rites

For Hindus, death is not the end of a person. It is when the soul (atman) leaves the body. The body is not needed any more and the soul is set free to continue into the next life.

When a Hindu dies, the funeral takes place as soon as possible after the death – on the same day if the person has died before sunset. This is to help stop disease spreading in a hot climate. The dead body is washed and prepared for the funeral. Men look after the body if the dead person is male, and women if the body is female. Most Hindus are cremated (the body is burned), but some are buried.

The body is wrapped in new cloth, as a sign of getting ready for something new. Then, it is carried out of the village to the cremation ground. If the Hindu lived in the UK or another Western country, then they would be taken to the local crematorium by car. The eldest son leads everyone to the cremation. If there are no sons, the nearest male relative will lead everyone.

The funeral pyre is a fire made of sweet-smelling wood. The eldest son starts by walking around the wood pile three times. The body, in its cloth, is placed on top of the wood pile and then more wood is added to cover it. Then the son lights the fire to cremate the body. Hindus believe that cremation helps the soul to escape from the body so that it is free to move on and be reborn as another person.

Everyone at the funeral stays until the body has been cremated. Afterwards, they go home to wash and change their clothes. The eldest son returns to the cremation ground a day or two after the funeral, to collect the ashes. These are then sprinkled in the River Ganges, if possible, as this is a very holy place for Hindus. Many Hindus believe that spreading the ashes in the Ganges helps the person who has died to achieve a better rebirth.

After the funeral, people make offerings to help the soul find a new body in which to live. Prayers are said for the dead, and relatives come to visit. The eldest son has

When a Hindu dies, the body is cremated on a funeral pyre.

a special role to play in all of this. He has to make sure that the funeral and the offerings are done properly. One of the reasons why Hindus like to have sons is so that their sons can take care of their funeral and make sure it is done in the right way. They believe this will help them to be reborn in a better life.

To people who are not Hindus, it must seem very hard to have a funeral in which everyone watches as the body of someone they loved is cremated. People in the West are more used to funerals where the body is not seen. But Hindus say that the funeral helps the relatives to come to terms with death, because they can see for themselves that the person really has died. They can see that the body has become empty and is not needed any more.

Discussion

Do you think a Hindu funeral would help relatives to come to terms with a death? Or do you think it would not be helpful? Give reasons for your answer.

Activity

1 Describe a Hindu funeral. Explain what the eldest son does, and say something about the funeral pyre.

2 Explain Hindu beliefs about what happens to someone's soul after they have died.

Muslim beliefs about heaven and hell

Muslims believe that this life is a test. They believe that when you die you stay in the grave until the Day of Judgement – **Yawmuddin**. On this day everyone will be raised from their graves. True followers of Allah will be 'reborn' in Paradise. Life after death is called **Akhirah**.

Surah 39 of the Qur'an says that on the Day of Judgement there will be the sound of a trumpet, and people will fall down as if they were unconscious. Then the dead will rise to join the living.

All people who believe in God will be judged at the last day.

> Those who believe (in the Qur'an), those who follow the Jewish (scriptures), and the Sabians and the Christians – any, who believe in Allah and the Last Day, and work righteousness – on them shall be no fear, Nor shall they grieve.
>
> (Surah 5:69)

Islam says that it is impossible to describe the afterlife but Muslims do believe that it lasts forever.

People who follow the words of Allah will live happily in a wonderful garden, **al-Janna** (Paradise):

> On the Day that the Hour will be established – that Day shall (all men) be sorted out. Then those who have believed and worked righteous deeds, shall be made happy in a Mead of Delight. And those who have rejected Faith and falsely denied Our Signs and the meeting of the Hereafter – such shall be brought forth to punishment.
>
> (Surah 30:14–16)

People who have not followed Allah's wishes will go to the fires of Hell – **Jahannam** – where they will be punished.

A Muslim graveyard

Allah is always merciful and even a bad person may eventually reach Paradise after they have been punished. The only crime that cannot be forgiven is **shirk**. Shirk means regarding something as being equal to Allah (see pages 39 and 190).

Moral behaviour and life after death

Muslims believe that you only have one chance at life and you are judged on how you live it. This Surah of the Qur'an describes judgement:

> To Allah belongs the Mystery of the heavens and the earth. And the Decision of the Hour (of Judgement) is as the twinkling of an eye, or even quicker: for Allah hath power over all things.
>
> (Surah 16:77)

Muslims believe that they will be judged according to how well they followed the teachings of the Qur'an and the example of Muhammad ﷺ (see page 94).

When Allah makes his judgement, he will look at what people have done and also what they intended to do (niyyah):

> If a person intends to do something wrong but does not do it, this is a good deed.
>
> If a person intends to do something wrong and does it, this is a bad deed.
>
> If a person intends to do a good deed but cannot manage to carry it out, this is a good deed.
>
> If a person intends a good deed and carries it out, this is equal to ten good deeds.
>
> (Hadith)

Everyone is responsible for his or her own actions because we all have free will. People can choose whether to follow the teachings of Islam but if they do not they will face the consequences at the Day of Judgement.

The Qur'an says that when the Last Judgement occurs it will be too late for people to repent.

Discussion

Do you consider that what you intend to do is as important as what you actually do?

Activity

Write a sentence about each of the following:

(a) *Day of Judgement*

(b) *Akhirah*

(c) *Paradise*

(d) *Hell*.

Glossary words

Yawmuddin

Akhirah

al-Janna

Jahannam

shirk

Muslim funeral rites

When they are dying, Muslims try to repeat the final words of the Prophet Muhammad ﷺ : 'Allah, help me through the hardship and agony of death'. When another Muslim hears about a death they will say, 'To Allah we belong and to Allah we return'.

Funerals take place within three days of death (if possible within 24 hours). The body is put on a stretcher with the head facing Makkah. Ritual washing (ghusl) is carried out by female relatives of the dead person if it is a woman and by male relatives if the dead person is a man. The body is washed three times and perfumed. It is wrapped in a shroud and placed in a coffin. If possible Muslims do not use a coffin (but in Britain burial without a coffin is not allowed). Muslims are buried facing Makkah.

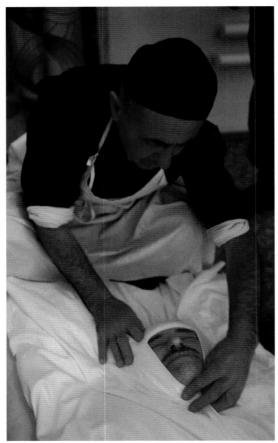

Muslims do not allow cremation, because they believe people will rise from the dead on the Day of Judgement. The Qur'an shows that Allah will put people back together on the Day of Judgement, from their bones, not from their ashes.

> Does man think that We cannot assemble his bones? Nay, We are able to put together in perfect order the very tips of his fingers.
>
> (Surah 75:3–4)

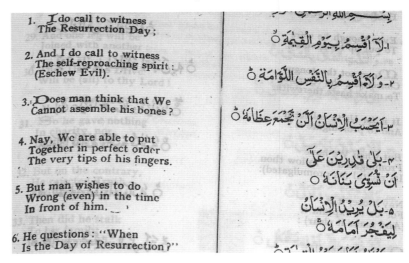

At the graveside people say Surah 1, **al-Fatihah**:

> In the name of Allah, Most Gracious, Most Merciful. Praise be to Allah, the Cherisher and Sustainer of the worlds; Most Gracious, Most Merciful; Master of the Day of Judgement. Thee do we worship, and Thine aid we seek. Show us the straight way. The way of those on whom Thou hast bestowed Thy Grace, those whose (portion) is not wrath, and who go not astray.

As the coffin is lowered into the ground, people say:

> From the (earth) did We create you, and into it shall We return you, and from it shall We bring you out once again.
>
> (Surah 20:55)

Graves are raised a little above the level of the ground to stop people walking or sitting on them.

Ritual washing of a dead Muslim

Carrying a coffin through the streets

Islam teaches that death should be accepted with trust and faith. The Prophet cried when his son died and it is natural for men and women to cry at a death. However, Muslims must remember that the death is the wish of Allah. Muslims ensure that mourners are not left on their own and will visit the family, bringing food.

Discussion

'Mourning and funeral services are for the living. They serve no purpose for the person who is dead.' What do you think about this statement?

Activity

1 What do Muslims believe about life after death?

2 Briefly describe a Muslim funeral.

Glossary words

al-Fatihah

 # Judaism

Jewish beliefs about life after death

Jews believe that G-d breathed the soul into Adam's body:

> ...and He blew into his nostrils the soul of life...
>
> (Genesis 2:7)

The **Midrash** says that the body cannot live without the soul, but neither can the soul live without the body. The rabbis said that the soul leaves the body during sleep and goes to heaven. It leaves the body again when someone dies but comes back to the body at resurrection. During Shabbat, Jews believe that G-d gives each body an extra soul, but takes it back at havdalah (the end of Shabbat).

Judaism says that Adam and Eve would have lived forever in the Garden of Eden but, because they disobeyed G-d, they became mortal and so, since then, everyone has grown old and eventually died.

When the Jewish scriptures were written, Jews believed that after death everyone went to **Sheol**. This is described as a dark place where people went after death and where they stayed for ever.

The first mention of life after death comes in the book of Daniel. This suggests that some people will be punished after death, and others will not:

> Many of those who sleep in the dusty earth will awaken: these for everlasting life and these for shame, for everlasting abhorrence.
>
> (Daniel 12:2)

Some Jews say that the good people will enter **Gan Eden** (Paradise) after death and that the wicked will go to **Gehenna** (Gehinnom). Gehenna is not the same as Sheol. Sheol was a place of waiting, while Gehenna is Hell. When someone is judged by G-d their body and soul will come together.

It is believed that this judgement will take place after the coming of the Messiah.

Moral behaviour and life after death

For a long time Jews believed that they would be punished for anything bad that their parents or grandparents had done.

> For I am HASHEM, your G-d – a jealous G-d, Who visits the sins of the fathers upon children to the third and fourth generations, for My enemies.
>
> (Exodus 20:5)

> Our fathers have sinned and are no more, and we have suffered for their iniquities.
>
> (Lamentations 5:7)

Later, they came to believe that it was how well they had lived their own lives that was important.

This passage says that G-d does not want people to believe they would be punished for what their parents had done (this is what the sentence about sour grapes means). Instead, each soul would be judged by itself:

> The word of HASHEM came to me, saying: Why do you relate this parable upon the land of Israel, saying, 'The fathers eat sour grapes, but the teeth of the sons are set on edge!' As I live – the word of the Lord HASHEM / ELOHIM – [I swear] that there will no longer be anyone among you who uses this parable in Israel. Behold, all souls are Mine, like the soul of the father, so the soul of the son, they are Mine. The soul that sins – it shall die.
>
> (Ezekiel 18:1–4)

Jews came to believe that there might be eternal life with G-d after death, but also that eventually G-d would judge people and that those who had not led good lives would go to hell.

The book of Maccabees describes how the Jews were persecuted by the Greeks. A man is being put to death because he refuses to say that he does not believe in G-d. He says that he would rather die because one day he will live with G-d:

> When he was near death, he said, 'One cannot but choose to die at the hands of mortals and to cherish the hope G-d gives of being raised again by him. But for you there will be no resurrection to life!'
>
> (2 Maccabees 7:14)

For Jews, the importance of life is the way in which it is lived on earth. Whatever may happen after death is in G-d's hands and should be left to G-d to arrange. To Jews, it is very important how they live their lives, not how this may affect their soul.

Jews must follow the Ten Commandments and the 613 mitzvot. They must live a **halakhic life** (walking with G-d) and treat others well. This is the most that anyone can do – it is left up to G-d to decide what, if anything, will happen next.

Discussion

'The only important thing is how you live your life, not what you believe.'

What do you think about this statement?

Activity

1 What do Jews believe about heaven and hell?

2 When will the day of judgement take place?

Glossary words

Midrash

Sheol

Gan Eden

Gehenna

halakhic life

The importance of life for Jews is the way in which it is lived on earth.

Jewish funeral rites

When they are dying Jews try to say the Shema:

> Hear, O Israel: HASHEM is our G-d, HASHEM, the One and Only. You shall love HASHEM, your G-d, with all your heart, with all your soul and with all your resources. Let these matters, which I command you today, be upon your heart. Teach them thoroughly to your children and speak of them while you sit in your home, while you walk on the way, when you retire and when you arise. Bind them as a sign upon your arm and let them be tefillin between your eyes. And write them on the doorposts of your house and upon your gates.

When someone dies, Jews say the **Kaddish**. This is often called the funeral prayer but it is really a prayer praising G-d.

> May His great Name grow exalted and sanctified in the world that He created as He willed. May He give reign to His kingship in your lifetime and in your days, and in the lifetimes of the entire Family of Israel, swiftly and soon. May His great Name be blessed forever and ever. Blessed, praised, glorified, exalted, extolled, mighty, upraised, and lauded be the Name of the Holy One, Blessed is He beyond any blessing and song, praise and consolation that are uttered in the world. May there be abundant peace from Heaven, and life, upon us and upon all Israel. He Who makes peace in His heights, may He make peace upon us, and upon all Israel.

Jews do not mourn for a long period. As soon as someone dies the burial must be arranged. If possible this will be on the same day, but if not then on the following one. The body is washed and dried and dressed in a simple white shroud. If the dead person is a man, the body is wrapped in a prayer shawl. The fringes are cut from the prayer shawl to show that the man is now freed from religious laws. All this is done by the **Chevra Kadisha** (Sacred Burial Society).

The body is put in a plain wooden coffin and this is sealed. The body is never left alone until the burial. Immediately before the burial the mourners will make a tear in their garments, **keriah**, to show their grief. No flowers are given at a Jewish funeral. This is because everyone is equal in death. If flowers were allowed, it would be an opportunity for rich families to have more flowers than the poor. Cremation is not usually allowed amongst Orthodox Jews.

After burial a blessing is said:

> May G-d comfort you among all the mourners of Zion and Jerusalem.

After the funeral the family will go home to sit Shiva. Shiva means 'seven'. For seven days a candle is kept burning and the mirrors in the house are covered. The mourners do not leave their homes, they do not shave or cut their hair and they sit on low stools. Kaddish is said three times a day. Shiva is broken only by the Sabbath or a Jewish festival. For thirty days the mourners do not go out for pleasure.

For the next eleven months (but no longer), Kaddish is said every day. After this the dead person is remembered each year on the anniversary of their death by the lighting of a **yahrzeit** candle and by the reciting of Kaddish.

Just before the first anniversary of the death, the tombstone will be placed at the grave and people often try to visit the graves of relatives during the High Holy Days, Rosh Hashanah and Yom Kippur. When people visit a Jewish grave they do not take flowers but instead place a small stone on the gravestone as a sign of respect.

Discussion

'Mourning and funeral services are for the living. They serve no purpose for the person who is dead.' What do you think about this statement?

Activity

Write a brief description of a Jewish funeral. Explain the importance of what happens.

Glossary words

Kaddish

Chevra Kadisha

keriah

yahrzeit

Practice GCSE questions

Christianity

(a) Describe Christian beliefs about life after death. (8 marks)

(b) Explain how a Christian funeral might help and comfort the relatives of someone who has died. (7 marks)

(c) 'If you behave badly in this life, you will be punished after you die.'
Do you agree? Give reasons to explain your answer, and show that you have thought about different points of view. You must refer to Christianity in your answer. (5 marks)

Hinduism

(a) Describe Hindu beliefs about life after death. (8 marks)

(b) Explain how a Hindu funeral might help and comfort the relatives of someone who has died. (7 marks)

(c) 'If you behave badly in this life, you will be punished after you die.'
Do you agree? Give reasons to explain your answer, and show that you have thought about different points of view. You must refer to Hinduism in your answer. (5 marks)

Islam

(a) Describe Muslim beliefs about life after death. (8 marks)

(b) Explain how a Muslim funeral might help and comfort the relatives of someone who has died. (7 marks)

(c) 'If you behave badly in this life, you will be punished after you die.'
Do you agree? Give reasons to explain your answer, and show that you have thought about different points of view. You must refer to Islam in your answer. (5 marks)

Judaism

(a) Describe Jewish beliefs about life after death. (8 marks)

(b) Explain how a Jewish funeral might help and comfort the relatives of someone who has died. (7 marks)

(c) 'If you behave badly in this life, you will be punished after you die.'
Do you agree? Give reasons to explain your answer, and show that you have thought about different points of view. You must refer to Judaism in your answer. (5 marks)

Tips

For all four questions

In part **(a)**, you are being asked to describe beliefs. Try to include as much detail as you can. You might want to explain what happens to good people and bad people. You may be able to say something about the holy books of the religion you are studying.

For part **(b)**, you need to think about how a funeral service might help people. What are the main beliefs that people remember at a funeral? They might be a way of telling the relatives that death is not the end. You might want to write about the comfort people might get just from having other family members and friends around them at a sad time.

In part **(c)**, you need to look at different points of view. Do you agree with the statement? Perhaps you think that bad people will be punished, through rebirth or as a result of being judged by God. Or you might think that death is just the end of a person, and that nothing else happens to them. Try to explain your own point of view, and compare it with the beliefs of the religion you are studying. If you agree with these beliefs, you will need to add another point of view as well, to show that you have considered different possibilities.

UNIT 5

Good and Evil

Christianity

Where does evil come from?

If there is a good God who can do anything at all, why do bad things happen? This is a question that Christians have often found hard to answer. Christians believe that God is perfectly good and perfectly loving. They also believe that God has the power to do anything (is **omnipotent**). But there are all kinds of bad things in the world. Sometimes people are cruel, or dishonest, or selfish – this is often called **moral evil**. It is the kind of wrong that happens because people choose to do it. At other times, bad things happen because of **natural evil** such as floods, disease, hurricanes, fires and earthquakes. Natural evil is the kind of wrong that is not anyone's fault. Life often seems very unfair. Terrible things sometimes happen to good people. Other people live bad lives but nothing seems to go wrong for them.

Do Christian beliefs about God make sense, if there is so much wrong in the world? Why doesn't God stop cruelty to children, or cancer, or tidal waves? Does God make bad things happen?

Different beliefs about God and the Devil

Some Christians believe that there is evil in the world because of the **Devil**, sometimes called **Satan**. They believe the Devil is the enemy of God. He rules in hell and tries to make people do wrong.

In the creation story in Genesis, Adam and Eve did wrong because a snake talked them into it. Some people believe that this was the Devil in disguise. In the book of Job, the Devil causes Job all sorts of suffering, as a way of trying to make him turn against God, but Job does not give up his faith.

Jesus was tempted by the Devil, but he refused to listen:

> Then the devil led him up and showed him in an instant all the kingdoms of the world. And the devil said to him ... 'If you, then, will worship me, it will all be yours.' Jesus answered him, 'It is written, "Worship the Lord your God, and serve only him."'
>
> (Luke 4:5–8)

In pictures, the Devil is shown as being red in colour, with horns and a forked tail. Some people say that all evil in the world comes from the Devil.

Not all Christians believe that the Devil is a real person. Some say that this is just a way of saying that people often want to do things even if they know they are wrong. Belief in the Devil does not provide a very good answer to the problem of evil. If God can do anything, why doesn't he stop the Devil?

Why does an all-powerful, all-loving God allow disasters to happen?

Some Christian responses to the problem of evil

Christians find it hard to explain why there is evil in the world. Sometimes, they say that it is the result of the Fall of Adam and Eve. The first people did not do what they were told by God. They spoilt the world that God had made. But this does not answer all the questions. Why didn't God make Adam and Eve so perfect that they would always choose the right thing? Didn't God know what they would do?

Other people say that evil and suffering are in the world as a kind of test, to help people to learn and become more mature. Some say that if people never suffered and never had to choose between right and wrong, then they would be like robots. Christians often say that suffering teaches important lessons. They say we could not be brave if we were never in danger, and we could not be kind if other people never needed anything. But not everyone agrees with this. People do not always learn good things when they suffer pain. It can make them angry and bitter.

Some Christians say that no-one knows why there is evil in the world. This is something that only God can understand. Christians believe that God does care about people when they suffer. Christians believe that Jesus was the Son of God, and that he came into the world and died on the cross. So God knows what pain is like and shares it with us. Sometimes, Christians say that when they suffer, they feel closer to God because they know they need God.

Discussion

Some people say that the existence of evil and suffering in the world proves that there is no God. Do you think this is fair?

Activity

1 (a) What do people call the sort of evil that is caused by humans doing wrong?

  (b) What do people call the sort of evil that happens naturally?

2 What might a Christian say about why there is evil in the world?

3 Do you think there can be a loving God, even though there is evil in the world? Give reasons for your answer.

Glossary words

omnipotent

moral evil

natural evil

Devil/Satan

How can Christians tell right from wrong?

Christians believe that they should try to become like God as much as they can. This means they should try to do the right thing, and keep away from doing wrong.

But how are they to know what is right and what is wrong?

There are different ways in which Christians can try to find out the right way to behave.

Conscience

Many people believe that they just know when something is right or wrong, because their **conscience** tells them. They feel guilty if they do something wrong, even if they know that no-one will find out about it. Sometimes they want to do something, but know that it would be wrong, and so they decide not to do it, because their conscience stops them. They know that they would not be happy if they acted against their conscience. Christians sometimes believe that the conscience is a way in which God speaks to them. Other people, however, do not agree with this. They think that the conscience comes from the way we are brought up. They think it is not God speaking to us – we are just remembering the things our parents told us.

The Bible

Christians often use the Bible to help them know right from wrong. They study the teachings of the Bible, and try to work out what it means for their own lives. Many people agree with the Bible about right and wrong, even if they are not Christians. A lot of people think the Ten Commandments are good rules for life, and a lot of people agree with the teaching of Jesus.

Many teachings and stories in the Bible have messages which Christians can try to put into practice. But this is not always easy. The Bible was written a long time ago. Some of the teachings of the Bible still mean the same thing today, such as 'Always treat other people in the way you would like to be treated' (Matthew 7:12). But other teachings are about things like how to look after slaves, or what to do if you argue with someone about an ox. It can be hard for modern people to see what these teachings might mean today.

Many Christians read the Bible when they have something important to decide.

The example of Christ

Sometimes, Christians try to work out the right thing to do by thinking about what Jesus would have done. Because Christians believe that Jesus was the Son of God, they believe that he always acted and spoke in the right way. They try to copy him. They might read in the Gospels about the ways in which Jesus helped the poor, and try to copy this by working in a shelter for the homeless, for example.

Why do Christians try to follow a moral code?

Christians believe that God is perfectly good. They believe that people were made 'in the image of God' (Genesis 1:27), so that they could share in God's goodness. Christians say that God has given people moral rules to follow, which are written in the Bible.

The Old Testament contains lots of rules about right and wrong. The teaching of Jesus, too, was often about right and wrong. Jesus sometimes taught in **parables**, which are stories that give a message. One famous example is the Parable of the Good Samaritan, by which Jesus taught that people should love each other like neighbours, even if they are strangers or from a different race (Luke 10:25–37). Another is the Parable of the Prodigal Son, which is about being sorry and being forgiven. The **Sermon on the Mount** (Matthew 5–7) contains a lot of Jesus' teaching about the right way to live. It covers a lot of topics, such as anger, adultery, divorce, and how to treat enemies.

Some Christians believe that people who try to be good in this life will be rewarded after death. People used to believe that good people go to heaven and bad people go to hell. But this view is not as popular today.

Discussion

Why should people do good and not evil? Is there any point in being good, unless you believe in God?

Activity

1 (a) Explain what people mean by the word *conscience*.

(b) Do you think that it is always right to do what your conscience tells you to do?

2 (a) How do Christians use the Bible to help them tell right from wrong?

(b) How do Christians use the example of Jesus to help them know what to do?

Glossary words

conscience

parables

Sermon on the Mount

Hinduism

Why is there evil in the world?

Hinduism teaches that God contains everything: making and destroying, light and darkness, birth and death, good and evil. Sometimes gods are shown in more than one form, because there are different sides to them. For example, the goddess Kali is seen as a mother; but at the same time, she is often shown as a frightening goddess. She has a necklace of skulls and she carries a human head. Shiva is sometimes shown as a quiet saint, but usually he is shown as 'Lord of the Dance', in a circle of flames. He destroys things and carries a thunderbolt. He rides through the world in his chariot, stirring up trouble. Hindus often blame Shiva for natural disasters such as earthquakes, floods and hurricanes.

For Hindus, good and evil are parts of life that come from God, just like light and shade or birth and death. Sometimes, Hindus try to keep the gods happy so that the gods will bring good luck and not bad luck. But often Hindus say that good and bad can be part of the same thing, depending on how you look at it. Sometimes the same event can bring good for some people while it brings harm for others.

The doctrine of karma and rebirth

Hindus believe that each person has an eternal soul or spirit, called **Atman**. This is born in one person, and after he or she dies it is reborn into another person (**rebirth,** or **reincarnation**). In each life, a person does good deeds and bad deeds. Everything a person does brings its own

The goddess Kali shows that both good and evil are aspects of God.

rewards and punishments, and this is called the law of **karma**.

When we look at the people around us, we can see that it does not always happen that good people are rewarded for what they do, or that bad people are punished. Hindus say that the reward or the punishment does not always come in this life. It might come in a future life – the good person, for example, might be born rich next time.

When bad things happen to people, Hindus do not think it is unfair. A Hindu would say it is because of the person's past lives, as a result of karma. Nothing happens by accident, and if someone is suffering, it is their own fault because of the things they have done in the past.

How do Hindus cope with evil and suffering?

Hindus believe that it is wrong to care too much for the pleasures that the world can bring. They try to remember the endless cycle of birth, death and rebirth, known as **samsara**. Hindus try to see that nothing in the world lasts for ever.

When Hindus suffer, they try to remember:
- Everything passes. Suffering will not last forever. The next life might bring more rewards and less pain.
- Suffering happens because of actions in past lives. Even if the person in pain is a small baby, this is not unfair, because the baby must have done something in a past life to deserve it.

Hindus try to cope with pain and suffering by loving God more. Loving God is known as **bhakti**. Making offerings, saying prayers and fasting will bring rewards in the future. Hindus believe that suffering is something that they can change by the way they behave.

Discussion

Do you think it is possible to be too attached to your family, or your home, or your friends, or your possessions? Give reasons for your answer.

Activity

1 Some people say that blaming suffering on past lives makes people have a hard attitude to the poor. It is like saying that it serves them right. What do you think, and why?

2 Explain what Hindus try to remember when they are suffering.

Glossary words

Atman

rebirth/reincarnation

karma

samsara

bhakti

How do Hindus know what is the right way to behave?

Hindus have different ideas about the right way to behave. A lot of their ideas about right and wrong come from the way they understand **dharma**. Dharma is an eternal law of right and wrong for everybody, even the gods. Dharma teaches that there are different ways of behaving that are right for different people. For example, there is a dharma for daughters, and another for wives, and another for widows. Men's dharma is different from women's dharma.

Hindu society is divided into different groups, known as **varnas**, and each of the different groups has its own rules. There is a dharma for Brahmins (the priestly class), another for Kshatriyas (the warrior class), another for Vaishyas (merchants), and another for Sudras (servants).

- **Brahmins** should be pure, read the holy books, be priests, and have self-control.
- **Kshatriyas** should be loyal, brave in battle, generous, and good leaders.
- **Vaishyas** should work hard in trade and farming, and look after other people. They should be honest and fair.
- **Sudras** should be servants for others. They should work hard and not be proud.

Sacred writings

Hindu books are often about right and wrong. Two of the most popular Hindu stories are the **Ramayana** and the **Mahabharata**. These tell long tales in which sometimes the main characters have to choose between right and wrong. The stories show how the characters behave, and what happens as a result. Hindus read these stories, tell them to their children, and act them out in plays. The morals of the stories help Hindus to understand right and wrong. They can try to be like the heroes, such as Lakshmana in the Ramayana, who was a brave and

loyal brother, or they can try to be like Sita, who was a good and faithful wife.

The **Bhagavad Gita** teaches about dharma. In the Bhagavad Gita, Arjuna is a Kshatriya (a man from the warrior class). His duty is to fight in battles. But in the story, the battle is between two parts of the same family. Arjuna does not want to fight because he does not want to kill his own family. Krishna teaches him that it is his duty, according to dharma, to be a warrior. He should do what is right for him, and not try to follow a different path:

> Think thou also of thy duty and do not waver. There is no greater good for a warrior than to fight in a righteous war.
>
> (Bhagavad Gita 2:31)

> And do thy duty, even if it be humble, rather than another's, even if it be great.
>
> (Bhagavad Gita 3:35)

The **Laws of Manu** is another piece of Hindu writing which contains a lot of teaching about right and wrong. Hindu tradition says it was written by Manu, the first man. It contains teachings on many topics, and Hindus might use it if they could not decide what to do.

Some Hindus follow the advice of a **guru**. Gurus are holy people who have studied the Vedas and who are believed to be very wise. Sometimes they use the stars to help them when they are giving advice.

Why do Hindus think it is important to try to be good?

Hindus believe that their behaviour in this life affects what will happen to them in future lives, because of the law of karma. If they do wrong, then in the future they might be born into a poor family, or be ill or disabled. If they follow their dharma and do the right thing, then they will have rewards in the future, with good health, lots of money and many sons.

The Bhagavad Gita teaches Hindus how to follow their dharma, or right path in life. Kshatriyas should fight in battles, because this is their dharma.

Hindus also try to be good as a way of pleasing the gods. A person who studies the holy books and does what is right will help the family to have good luck, because the gods will be pleased.

Discussion

Do you agree that our behaviour in this life affects the way we are reborn?

What do you think are the best reasons for leading a good life?

Activity

1 What do Hindus mean by the word *dharma*?

2 Why do Hindus think it is important to be good in this life?

Glossary words

dharma

varnas

Brahmins

Kshatriyas

Vaishyas

Sudras

Ramayana

Mahabharata

Bhagavad Gita

Laws of Manu

guru

Beliefs about the goodness of Allah and the nature of Shaytan/'Iblis

Islam believes that Allah is good and merciful:

> In the name of Allah, Most Gracious, Most Merciful. Praise be to Allah, the Cherisher and Sustainer of the worlds: Most Gracious, Most Merciful.
>
> (Surah 1:1–3)

Muslims believe that Allah will look after them and guide them in their life. There is evil and suffering in the world, but Allah will protect people if they choose to follow Islam. The reason there is evil and suffering is because of **Shaytan** – the Devil. Shaytan is also called **'Iblis**.

Islam teaches that Allah made the first man, Adam, from clay. He also made angels (called **mala'ikah**) from light, and he made spirits out of fire. These spirits were called **Jinn**. After Allah had made Adam, he told the angels and the Jinn to bow down to him. The angels obeyed but one of the Jinn refused. This Jinn was called 'Iblis.

> (Allah) said: 'O 'Iblis! What is your reason for not being among those who prostrated themselves?' ('Iblis) said: 'I am not one to prostrate myself to man, whom Thou didst create from sounding clay, from mud moulded into shape'. (Allah) said: 'Then get thee out from here: for thou art rejected, accursed. And the Curse shall be on thee till the Day of Judgement'.
>
> (Surah 15:32–35)

'Iblis said that he would tempt humans to do wrong rather than right. This is where evil and suffering come from. Allah allows Shaytan to tempt people. Shaytan cannot make people do wrong, because Allah has given everyone free will. This means that people can choose to follow Allah's will – or not.

Shaytan is not equal to Allah and he cannot harm people unless Allah allows it:

> But he cannot harm them in the least, except as Allah permits; and on Allah let the Believers put their trust.
>
> (Surah 58:10)

'Iblis is sometimes called Shaytan – the Devil. In his last sermon, Muhammad ﷺ warned his followers:

> Beware of Shaytan, he is desperate to divert you from the worship of Allah, so beware of him in matters of your religion.

In the Qur'an it says that Adam and Hawwa' (Eve) were tempted by Shaytan and ate the fruit of the forbidden tree in Al-Jannah (Paradise). Allah forgave Adam and Hawwa' their sins when they prayed to him. Adam and Hawwa' begged for Allah's mercy:

> Our Lord! We have wronged our own souls: if Thou forgive us not and bestow not upon us Thy Mercy, we shall certainly be lost.
>
> (Surah 7:23)

Allah said that they were forgiven, and that he would protect all people who followed him:

> Get ye down all from here: and if, as is sure, there comes to you guidance from Me, whosoever follows My guidance, on them shall be no fear, nor shall they grieve.
>
> (Surah 2:38)

For Muslims, life is a series of tests. Because Allah has given humans free will, they have the chance to prove their faith in Allah. Those who follow Allah's will even while they are suffering will be blessed by Allah:

> Be sure we shall test you with something of fear and hunger, some loss in goods or lives or the fruits (of your toil), but give glad tidings to those who patiently persevere – who say, when afflicted with

calamity: 'To Allah we belong, and to Him is our return' – They are those on whom (descend) blessings from their Lord, and Mercy, and they are the ones that receive guidance.

(Surah 2:156–157)

Muslims believe that there is life after death and the next life will be better than this one. Muslims should try to stop other people from suffering:

What is the life of this world but amusement and play? But verily the Home in the Hereafter – that is life indeed, if they but knew.

(Surah 29:64)

Discussion

How do you think a Muslim might cope with suffering if it seems that prayers are not answered?

Activity

Write a short paragraph explaining why 'Iblis disobeyed Allah, and what happened.

Glossary words

Shaytan/'Iblis

mala'ikah

Jinn

Living according to the will of Allah

Muslims believe that all human beings are born without sin (**fitrah**). Muslims can choose whether to do what Allah wants. Although Muslims can make their own decisions, Allah already knows what these decisions will be. In order to obey Allah people must make the right decisions.

Allah forgives people who admit that they are wrong and ask to be forgiven. Islam says that good is always better than evil:

> Nor can Goodness and Evil be equal. Repel (Evil) with what is better. Then will he between whom and thee was hatred become as it were thy friend and intimate!
>
> (Surah 41:34)

Islam means 'submission' and living according to the Five Pillars, the teachings of the Qur'an and the example of Muhammad ﷺ. It is living according to Allah's will.

The Five Pillars are at the centre of a Muslim's life:

- **Shahadah** – a statement of faith which states:

  There is no god except Allah, Muhammad is the Messenger of Allah.

- **Salah** – five daily prayers to worship and speak to Allah. These are done in the way that the Prophet Muhammad ﷺ taught and are said in Arabic. Saying these prayers means that at regular intervals work has to stop and Muslims have the chance to focus their thoughts on Allah.

- **Zakah** – this means 'the purification of wealth by the payment of an annual welfare due'. Muslims give 2.5% of their spare money as Zakah. This prevents them from being greedy or thinking about money too much.

- **Hajj** – pilgrimage to Makkah. All Muslims who are fit and can afford it should take part in the annual pilgrimage to Makkah once in their lives. This gives people the chance to do what Allah wants and also to visit the holy places of Islam.

- **Sawm** – fasting during Ramadan. Fasting during Ramadan is very important for Muslims because they have the chance of

thinking about Allah and sharing the experience with their families and with the **ummah** (the world-wide community of Muslims).

Islam brings together belief and everyday life and helps people in their relationship with God.

The Qur'an and the teachings and example of Muhammad ﷺ help Muslims to make decisions about their life. They give Muslims a clear idea of how Allah wishes them to behave. They provide Muslims with the examples they need to determine 'right' from 'wrong'.

Living in submission to Allah is the way a Muslim would want to live because it shows respect to Allah and shows that the Muslim is grateful for Allah's love and care.

Discussion

Do you think people could still have free choice, even if Allah has planned their lives?

Activity

Write brief notes about each of the Five Pillars, showing why they are important for Muslims.

Glossary words

fitrah

Shahadah

Salah

Zakah

Hajj

Sawm

ummah

Judaism

Beliefs about the goodness of G-d and the nature of Satan

Jews believe that G-d is good and will always protect and care for them.

Because he is good, G-d created the world and gave the Israelites the Ten Commandments so that they would know how to live. Also G-d saved the Israelites from their enemies and made agreements (covenants) with them.

> And I will make of you a great nation;
> I will bless you, and make your name great, and you shall be a blessing. I will bless those who bless you, and him who curses you I will curse; and all the families of the earth shall bless themselves by you.
>
> (Genesis 12:2–3)

Judaism believes that when G-d created humans he made them so that they could choose whether to worship him or not. G-d would not want people to worship him like robots. People must follow G-d's teachings because they want to.

But because people are free to choose, they sometimes make the wrong choices. This may mean that they suffer:

> Not to have known suffering is not to be truly human.
>
> (Midrash)

Judaism says that good people suffer for their sins but will be rewarded in paradise. Wicked people are rewarded for any good they have done but they will be punished when they die.

Good and evil

A Jewish story says that when G-d decided to create human beings he asked the angels about it. Some of them thought it was a good idea but others said that this would lead to arguments. G-d did decide to create human beings.

The angels wanted to worship Adam but the man pointed to G-d. All the angels were told to bow down to Adam but Satan refused and was thrown down into hell.

The idea of good and evil begins in the Torah with the story of Adam and Eve in the Garden of Eden:

> HASHEM G-d took the man and placed him in the Garden of Eden, to work it and to guard it. And HASHEM G-d commanded the man, saying, 'Of every tree of the garden you may freely eat, but of the Tree of Knowledge of Good and Bad, you must not eat thereof; for on the day you eat of it, you shall surely die.'
>
> (Genesis 2:15–17)

> Now the serpent was cunning beyond any beast of the field that HASHEM G-d had made. He said to the woman, 'Did, perhaps, G-d say: "You shall not eat of any tree of the garden?"' The woman said to the serpent, 'Of the fruit of any tree of the garden we may eat. Of the fruit of the tree which is in the centre of the garden G-d has said: "You shall neither eat of it nor touch it, lest you die."' The serpent said to the woman, 'You will not surely die; for G-d knows that on the day you eat of it your eyes will be opened and you will be like G-d, knowing good and bad.' And the woman perceived that the tree was good for eating and that it was a delight to the eyes, and that the tree was desirable as a means to wisdom, and she took of its fruit and ate; and she gave also to her husband with her and he ate.
>
> (Genesis 3:1–6)

Satan first appears in the book of Chronicles, where he is seen trying to influence King David:

> An adversary [Satan] stood against Israel, and enticed David to take a count of [the people of] Israel.
>
> (1 Chronicles 21:1)

In the Book of Job, Satan is seen as a spy for G-d who travels around the earth and reports everyone whom he sees behaving badly. G-d allows him to do this but sets limits on his power.

Sins and punishment

At first Jews believed that people were punished for things which their parents or grandparents had done wrong:

For I am Hashem, your G-d – a jealous G-d, Who visits the sins of the fathers upon children to the third and fourth generations, for My enemies; but Who shows kindness for thousands [of generations] to those who love Me and observe My commandments.

(Exodus 20:5–6)

But later the prophet Ezekiel said that people could only be punished for their own sins:

Behold, all souls are Mine, like the soul of the father, so the soul of the son, they are Mine. The soul that sins – it shall die.

(Ezekiel 18:4)

Coping with suffering

Since the Jews were driven out of Israel in 70 CE they have suffered from persecution many times in many countries. Although Jewish people have suffered so much, Jews always try to accept what happens to them as G-d's will. The story of Job in the Torah is an example for religious Jews. Despite terrible suffering, Job never loses his faith in G-d. At the end of the story, G-d rewards him.

Jews believe that they should apologise to G-d and to other people for their behaviour every year, in preparation for Yom Kippur, the Day of Atonement. They say sorry for all the Jewish people, not just for their own mistakes.

Discussion

Do you think that it really matters whether the stories of Adam and Eve and of the fall of Lucifer (Satan) are true?

Activity

Explain what happened in the Garden of Eden. Why were Adam and Eve forced to leave?

The Holocaust

Throughout history the Jews have been persecuted and have suffered for their religion. Jews see suffering as a test of their faith in G-d.

Jews suffered from the Egyptians and the Babylonians and, later, from the Greeks and the Romans.

Most Jews were driven out of Israel in the first century CE and Israel did not become a Jewish homeland again until 1948. For 900 years Jews lived all over the world.

The most recent disaster to hit the Jews was the **Shoah** or **Holocaust** of the Second World War. The Chancellor of Germany, Adolf Hitler, told his people that he was going to create the **'Master Race'**. These would be Aryan people, tall with blonde hair and blue eyes. In an event called the **Final Solution**, Hitler tried to destroy all the Jews in Europe. Millions of Jews were collected together in camps in Germany and Poland, such as Auschwitz–Birkenau, Sobibór and Treblinka, and here they were gassed or starved to death. Six million Jews were murdered. The Nazis also murdered other groups of people whom they thought were a 'problem' – like communists, homosexuals, gypsies and Slavs.

Although millions died, Hitler was not successful and after his defeat Judaism began to grow once more.

Some Jews felt that their G-d had let them down. Many Jews did say that 'G-d died in Auschwitz', or that 'G-d was not in Auschwitz'. Other Jews believed that, despite this disaster, 'G-d was in Auschwitz' caring for his people.

Making moral decisions

The teachings in the Torah and the Talmud show Jews how to lead an **halakhic life** – a life of walking with G-d. This way of life means following the Ten Commandments and the 613 **mitzvot**.

The rules and regulations in the Bible are not put there to make life difficult. They are a guide and a set of instructions as to how G-d wants his people to live.

This is the gateway to the Nazi concentration camp at Auschwitz–Birkenau. The sign on the gate says 'Work Makes You Free'.

G-d made covenants (agreements) with Noah, Abraham, Moses and Jeremiah.

Some of these are one-sided. G-d simply says what he will do. This happened with Noah after the flood:

> And I will confirm My covenant with you: Never again shall all flesh be cut off by the waters of the flood, and never again shall there be a flood to destroy the earth.
>
> (Genesis 9:11)

The later covenants say what G-d will do and what he expects his people to do. When he promises to make Abraham the founder of a great nation, he says:

> And as for you, you shall keep My covenant – you and your offspring after you throughout the generations. This is My covenant which you shall keep between Me and you and your offspring after you: Every male among you shall be circumcised.
>
> (Genesis 17:9–10)

The first commandment was given to Adam when G-d told him to:

> Be fruitful and multiply, fill the earth and subdue it.
>
> (Genesis 1:28a)

Judaism says that as well as giving Moses the written Torah (the five books: Genesis, Exodus, Leviticus, Numbers and Deuteronomy), G-d also gave him the oral Torah. The oral Torah explained the teachings of the written Torah.

The oral Torah was later written down and became the Talmud. The Talmud also contains the teachings of many rabbis, explaining the Law.

Jews use the Torah and Talmud to help them make decisions. These sacred writings tell Jews how to know good from evil, and how to live a good life.

Discussion

Is there any way in which the enormous suffering of the Holocaust can be explained and understood?

Activity

Write a sentence about each of the covenants mentioned on this page.

Glossary words

Shoah/Holocaust

'Master Race'

Final Solution

halakhic life

mitzvot

Practice GCSE questions

Christianity

(a) Describe Christian beliefs about why there is evil in the world. (8 marks)

(b) Explain how a Christian might find out the right way to behave. (7 marks)

(c) 'People should try to be happy; there is no point in trying to be good.'
Do you agree? Give reasons to support your answer, and show that you have thought about different points of view. You must refer to Christianity in your answer. (5 marks)

Hinduism

(a) Describe Hindu beliefs about why there is evil in the world. (8 marks)

(b) Explain how a Hindu might find out the right way to behave. (7 marks)

(c) 'People should try to be happy; there is no point in trying to be good.'
Do you agree? Give reasons to support your answer, and show that you have thought about different points of view. You must refer to Hinduism in your answer. (5 marks)

Islam

(a) Describe Muslim beliefs about why there is evil in the world. (8 marks)

(b) Explain how a Muslim might find out the right way to behave. (7 marks)

(c) 'People should try to be happy; there is no point in trying to be good.'
Do you agree? Give reasons to support your answer, and show that you have thought about different points of view. You must refer to Islam in your answer. (5 marks)

Judaism

(a) Describe Jewish beliefs about why there is evil in the world. (8 marks)

(b) Explain how a Jew might find out the right way to behave. (7 marks)

Tips

For all four questions

In part **(a)**, you need to describe the beliefs of the religion you are studying, rather than giving your own opinion. What might a religious believer say about evil and suffering in the world? Would they blame it on God, or the Devil, or on people? What reasons would they give? For high marks, you should try to explain religious ideas as clearly as you can, and perhaps give some examples.

In part **(b)**, you should show your understanding. Try to think of several different ideas. You might write about the holy books and the traditions of the religion you are studying. You might write about examples people might follow.

For part **(c)**, you need to show that you understand people might have different views about this. What might a religious believer say about why people should bother to be good? What might a non-believer, or someone from a different religion, say to this question? Remember to give your own view, too. It might be the same as one of the ideas you have already given, or it might be another, different point of view.

(c) 'People should try to be happy; there is no point in trying to be good.'
Do you agree? Give reasons to support your answer, and show that you have thought about different points of view. You must refer to Judaism in your answer. (5 marks)

UNIT 6

Religion and Human Relationships

Unit 6 Religion and Human Relationships

Christianity

Christian marriage ceremonies

Christians believe that a marriage should be for life, if possible. In a Christian marriage, the priest, vicar or minister begins by explaining that marriage was made by God. The bride and groom agree in front of everyone that they are free to marry each other, and it is their own choice. Then they make promises, or vows. In these vows, they promise to love and comfort each other, to honour each other, to support each other whatever happens and to be faithful to each other for the rest of their lives. They give each other rings, and the marriage is blessed. There are prayers and hymns. The bride and groom sign the marriage register to make the marriage legal.

Wedding customs in Christianity are different in different parts of the world. The bride often wears a white dress as a sign of being pure. She often has bridesmaids who help her with her dress and her flowers. Sometimes confetti is thrown, or sweets are given to the guests, or money is pinned to the bride. Christian marriages show Christian beliefs about why marriage is important:

● They show the belief that marriage is something made by God.
● They show that men and women should have a Christian marriage because of their own free choice, and not because someone else has forced them into it.
● They show the Christian belief in **monogamy** (a faithful partnership between one man and one woman). They also show that a Christian marriage is meant to be for life.

● They show the belief that the best way for children to be brought up is with two parents who are married for life.

Discussion

Do you think people should plan to stay married for life? Try to support your answer with reasons.

Christians believe that marriage is part of God's plan for people. It should be for life.

102

The roles of men and women within a Christian family

Christians have different views about the roles that men and women should have within a family. Some Christians believe that God planned men and women to have different roles. They say that men and women are just as important as each other, but they were made for different reasons.

In the book of Genesis, the creation story tells how Adam was made first, and then Eve. Eve was made because God did not want Adam to be lonely:

> The LORD God said, 'It is not good for the man to be alone. I will make a helper suitable for him.'
>
> (Genesis 2:18)

Christians sometimes say that this shows that women are meant to be helpers for men. The duties of a man come first, and the woman should support him, because that was why she was made in the first place. Some Christians say that women are weaker than men and are more likely to do wrong, because Eve did wrong before Adam. So they might think the man should be the leader, and the woman should do what he says.

In the New Testament, 1 Peter (a letter written to a newly formed Christian church) says:

> Wives, ... be submissive to your husbands ... Husbands, in the same way be considerate as you live with your wives, and treat them with respect as the weaker partner.
>
> (1 Peter 3:1,7)

Some Christians say that these teachings are still true today. They might say that a woman should have a different role from a man when they are married. She should look after the home, take care of the children, and support her husband in his career. If, for example, her husband is offered a good job which means moving house, she should be willing to go, if this is what he thinks is right.

Other Christians say that these views belong in the past. They say that men and women were made equal; they were both made 'in the image of God'. If a married couple have children, both the mother and the father should share child-care. Both partners should be able to go out to work if this is what they want to do. Some parts of the Bible seem to agree with this point of view:

> There is neither ... male nor female, for you are all one in Christ Jesus.
>
> (Galatians 3:28)

Some Christian women think it is their role to do the child-care and housework, and support their husbands in their careers. Other Christian households have a more modern view, where men and women have more equal roles.

Discussion

Do you think that there are jobs at home, or in the world of work, that are more suitable for men or more suitable for women? Give reasons to support your argument.

Activity

1 Describe the main features of a Christian wedding ceremony.

2 Explain why Christians still believe that marriage is important. Try to give several reasons.

Glossary words

monogamy

Christian beliefs about divorce

All Christians know that sometimes marriages do not work, and a married couple might end up making each other unhappy. But there are very different views about what Christians should do if they no longer want to stay with the person they married.

The teaching in the Bible is not always clear about divorce. In Matthew's Gospel, Jesus teaches that a man is only allowed to divorce his wife if she has been unfaithful to him (Matthew 5:31–32), but in Mark's Gospel, divorce is not allowed at all (Mark 10:11–12). Christians do not agree about which is the right teaching to follow.

The **Roman Catholic Church** teaches that married couples may live apart, if that is what they want to do, but they may not divorce. Catholics believe that marriage is a **sacrament**. It is something holy that God has done, and it cannot be undone. Roman Catholics must not marry someone new if their first husband or wife is still alive.

Other Christian churches, such as the **Church of England**, have different ideas. They believe that divorce can be allowed, and both partners are then free to marry other people. It is up to the vicar to decide if they can get married in church when they have been divorced before.

The Christian churches agree that they should do all they can to help couples who have problems with their marriage. They often have special classes for people who are about to get married, and groups that married couples can join to talk about how they can work towards a happy married life.

Christian beliefs about sexual relationships

Within Christianity, there are many different opinions about sexual relationships. Many Christians believe that sex is only right if it is between people who are married to each other. This means that sex before marriage, homosexual relationships and affairs outside marriage are all wrong. They say that the Bible teaches that the human body is a 'temple of the Holy Spirit'. It should be treated with respect:

> Do you not know that your body is a temple of the Holy Spirit, who is in you, whom you have received from God? You are not your own; you were bought at a price. Therefore honour God with your body.
>
> (1 Corinthians 6:19)

Christians also say that God made sex for a reason, so that people could have children, and to make the love between married people stay strong. If sex is not used for the reasons God made it, then this spoils something that was meant to be very special.

Other Christians believe that these views are old-fashioned. They say that the main message of Christianity is love, and that if a relationship is loving, sex can be right even if the people are not married to each other.

Contraception (birth control)

The Roman Catholic Church teaches that artificial contraception is wrong. This means that it is wrong for people to stop pregnancy by using methods such as the Pill or condoms. 'Natural' methods of contraception are allowed, such as planning to have sex only at times of the month when the woman is less likely to get pregnant.

Roman Catholics teach this because they believe God made sex so that babies could be born. They think that when people have sex, there should always be the chance that a baby might be started.

Some people, however, including some Roman Catholics, disagree with this teaching. They say that it is wrong for poor people to have very large families if they have not got enough money and food for them.

Other Christian churches, such as the Church of England, teach that it is sensible for people to use contraception. They say people should be free to choose when to have children, and how many they want to have. Every child should be wanted by its parents.

Discussion

Why do you think couples today often choose to live together without getting married?

Do you think people should marry if they want to have children? Or doesn't it matter?

Activity

1 Explain different Christian views about divorce. Why do some Christians think it is wrong? Why do other Christians allow it?

2 Explain different Christian views about contraception. Why do some Christians think it is wrong? Why do other Christians allow it?

3 Do you think sex should only happen between people who are married to each other? Give reasons for your answer, and explain what a Christian might say.

Glossary words

Roman Catholic Church

sacrament

Church of England

Hinduism

Hindu marriage ceremonies

Hindus believe that marriage is an important duty for men and women. In Hinduism, a marriage does not just join together a man and a woman, but brings together two whole families. Hindu parents often arrange a marriage for their son or daughter, or help them by organising meetings with people who might make suitable partners.

Hindus have many different marriage customs. Weddings take place at a time chosen using horoscopes. In the bride's home, cooking and parties will begin several days before the wedding. The wedding ceremony can take place in the home of the bride, but often a hall is hired with room for lots of guests. A small altar is set up in the middle. The bride and her family wait in the hall to welcome the groom and his relations. Blessings are said and sung by the two families and the priest. Then the bride is given away in marriage by her parents, who join the couple's hands. The priest lights a holy fire. He says sacred chants, called **mantras**, in the holy language of Sanskrit. The groom repeats the holy words which ask for the marriage to be blessed with children. The end of the bride's sari is tied to her new husband's scarf, to show that they are joined together.

Often, the bride places her foot on a stone, to show that she will perform her duties as a wife. Then the couple walk seven steps around the sacred fire, with the groom's right hand on the bride's right shoulder, and at every step a prayer is said for a special blessing:

1 for food
2 for strength
3 for wealth
4 for wisdom and happiness
5 for children
6 for good health
7 for friendship.

The 'seven steps' around the sacred fire are the most important part of a Hindu marriage.

Everyone blesses the couple with good wishes for a long, happy marriage with children and grandchildren.

These wedding customs show that in Hinduism, marriage is for life. The husband and wife have duties to one another, and have the support of the whole community.

The roles of men and women in a Hindu family

In Hinduism, men have been the leaders, not women. Today, Hindu women have more freedom, especially if they live in the West. But in Indian villages the roles of men and women are still very different. Hindus teach that everyone has his or her own **dharma** (sacred duty) to follow, and the dharma for a married man is different from the dharma for a married woman.

A woman's father looks after her until she gets married, and then her husband takes on that task. The birth of girls is often less welcome than the birth of boys, because girls need someone to pay for them. Often, a girl will be given less education than a boy, because the boy will have to look after his wife and perhaps also his parents in their old age. He needs to be able to earn a living. In India, Hindu women do not often have a career of their own. They work in the house, looking after their mother-in-law when they are first married, and then their own children later on. They take care of the **puja** (worship) in the home, and make sure that the house is clean and comfortable. Hindus think that being a mother is very important. Many Hindu women believe that having sons is the best thing that could happen to them.

Hindu men have important duties in the family. As sons, they have to do the religious duties at their parents' funerals. As husbands, they have a duty to be faithful to their wives and to work hard. They have to earn enough money to support other family members. Hindu men sometimes do housework, but this is usually seen as women's work.

Rama and Sita

Hindus think the god Rama and his wife Sita are the best example for married couples. In the Ramayana, Sita gave up a life of riches in the palace so that she could look after Rama when he was sent to live in the forest. Sita was always faithful to her husband, she was modest, and she did what Rama asked. Rama did all the duties of a good husband, by protecting Sita from harm and risking his own life to rescue her.

Discussion

Hindus sometimes say that young people are not in a very good position to choose a marriage partner. They have not been married before, and so do not know what to look for in a partner. What do you think about this point of view?

Activity

1 Write two or three sentences about Hindus and arranged marriages.

2 In a Hindu wedding ceremony, what do the seven steps around the fire mean?

3 Explain in your owns words what Hindus expect of married men, and what they expect of married women.

Glossary words

mantras

dharma

puja

Motherhood is greatly valued in Hinduism.

Hindu beliefs about divorce

Many Hindu marriages are arranged, so Hindus do not expect the same things that people in the West expect when they marry. The couple do not always think they will find life together easy. They know they will have to get to know each other slowly.

Hinduism teaches that marriage is for life. Once a couple has been joined together in the wedding ceremony, they are not meant to be divorced. But separation and divorce do happen. Men sometimes divorce their wives if they have not had a son after several years. In some Hindu societies, a Hindu woman brings shame on her husband and his family if she does not get on with them, or does not have children. She will be sent back to her father or brothers, who may try to find a second marriage partner for her. Many Hindu couples prefer to stay together even if they dislike each other, because everyone thinks divorce is such a bad thing.

Hindu attitudes towards sexual relationships

Kama, or physical pleasure, is one of the four aims of life for Hindus. Sex is believed to be a good thing, to be enjoyed. It is also one of the duties of married life, to produce sons. But Hinduism teaches that sex is only right between people who are married to each other.

Hindus disagree with sex before marriage. Young people are supposed to study Hindu teachings before they marry. Hindu parents watch their children very carefully, and usually do not allow them any contact with the opposite sex except for close family members, until they get married. This is seen as very important for girls. In India it is still quite common for girls to be married when they are in their teens, to make sure that they have

had no sexual experience before the wedding day.

Homosexuality is not mentioned at all in Hindu writing. It is treated in Hindu society as though it does not happen. Same-sex relationships are not even talked about.

In Hindu societies, it is usual for young people to mix only with members of the same sex, until they get married.

Hindu beliefs about contraception (birth control)

Hindus used to think that it was good to have as many children as possible. Adults needed to have children to help with the work. It was quite common for there to be as many as eight or ten children in a family, although not all of them would survive to become adults. Hindus think children are a great blessing. Hindu holy books tell people not to limit the number of children that they have.

But in modern times, things have changed. Children are more likely to live to be adults. The population of India has grown faster than that of many other countries. The Indian government has told people it is a good idea to use contraception and to limit their families to two or three children. Many Hindus use some form of birth control, but most want to keep having children until they get a boy. The government sends health workers into poorer areas to teach people about how to get and use contraceptives.

Discussion

Do you think it is all right for Hindus to value sons more highly than daughters? Or do you think something should be done to change that attitude?

Activity

1 Describe what life is like for many Hindu married women.

2 Why is divorce quite rare amongst Hindus?

3 Why does the Indian government try to help people keep their families small?

Glossary words

kama

Islam

Muslim marriage ceremonies

A Muslim marriage ceremony is very simple. There is a statement that the bride and groom have chosen to marry. The marriage contract is then signed. In the contract it says what dowry (usually a gift of money) the groom is giving to the bride. Then there are prayers and readings followed by a sermon.

> Almighty God created humanity, male and female, each in need of the other, and established the institution of marriage as a means of uniting souls in blessed bond of love...

The Qur'an says what a marriage should be:

> Among His signs it is that, that He created you from dust; and then – Behold, ye are human beings scattered (far and wide). And among His signs is this, that He created for you mates from among yourselves, that ye may dwell in tranquillity with them, and He has put love and mercy between your (hearts): verily in that are Signs for those who reflect.
>
> (Surah 30:20–21)

> They are your garments and ye are their garments.
>
> (Surah 2:187)

Marriage and the family are at the heart of Muslim life:

The Muslim marriage ceremony.

> It is He Who has created man from water: then has He established relationships of lineage and marriage.
>
> (Surah 25:54)

> No institution in Islam finds more favour with God than marriage.
>
> (Hadith)

Sometimes Muslim marriages are arranged by families. The couple are only allowed to meet each other when members of their families are present. In Islam, no-one can be forced to marry someone, and if this did happen then the marriage would be invalid – it would not count:

> The father or any other guardian cannot give in marriage a virgin or one who has been married before without her consent.
>
> (Hadith)

Men are told to be careful about who they marry:

> A woman is taken in marriage for three reasons; for her beauty, for family connections or the lure of wealth. Choose the one with faith and you will have success.
>
> (Hadith 4:235)

The roles of men and women within a Muslim family

Islam says that men and women are equal and that Allah will judge them equally.

To help men value women for who they are, rather than for their bodies, women wear garments that leave only the hands and face exposed (see Surah 33:59).

Islam says that men and women have the same rights and responsibilities but also that men and women are different. Men must support the family while women have children and bring them up. Women have many rights which are the same whether they are married or single:

- they can choose to study
- they can refuse to be married
- they can get a divorce
- they can inherit money or property
- they can keep their own names
- they can own property
- they can take part in politics.

Muhammad ﷺ taught the respect which should be shown to women:

> Paradise lies at the feet of your mother.
>
> (Sunan An-Nasa'i)

> A man asked Prophet Muhammad ﷺ, 'O Messenger of Allah! Who deserves the best care from me?' The Prophet said, 'Your mother.' The man asked, 'Who then?' The Prophet said, 'Your mother.' The man asked yet again, 'Who then?' Prophet Muhammad ﷺ said, 'Your mother.' The man asked once more, 'Who then?' The Prophet then said, 'Your father.'
>
> (Sahih Al-Bukhari)

The importance of a husband and wife living together is found in the Qur'an:

> Among His signs is this, that He created for you mates from among yourselves, that ye may dwell in tranquillity with them, and He has put love and mercy between your (hearts): verily in that are Signs for those who reflect.
>
> (Surah 30:21)

Men are expected to help at home, because Muhammad ﷺ helped his wives.

Discussion

Do you think there are jobs at home, or in the world of work, that are more suitable for one gender than for the other? Give reasons to support your argument.

Activity

Make a list of what Muslim women are allowed to do. Then compare your list with what you know about non-Muslim women.

Muslim beliefs about divorce

Muslims know that sometimes marriages break down. Marriages should be ended if the couple are miserable and this makes their children and family unhappy. The Hadith says that 'Among all lawful things, divorce is most hated by Allah'. However, divorce is allowed, and it is lawful.

The Qur'an says that:

> If a wife fears cruelty or desertion on her husband's part, there is no blame on them if they arrange an amicable settlement between themselves; and such settlement is best; even though men's souls are swayed by greed.
>
> (Surah 4:128)

A man cannot divorce his wife until it is certain that she is not pregnant. Once the divorce is announced he has to wait three months in the hope that they will work out their problems. After this the divorce takes place.

A woman can leave her marriage completely if she returns her dowry. During the three months of waiting she must stay in her husband's house and he must provide everything for her.

A woman can get a divorce, by agreeing this with her husband, or because of the way he has treated her.

Men and women can remarry after divorce. A couple can remarry each other if they divorce. They can do this two times. Islam does have rules about marrying people from other faiths. A Muslim man can marry a Jewish or Christian woman but a Muslim woman can only marry a Muslim.

Muslim beliefs about sexual relationships and contraception

Muslims believe that sexual intercourse is for pleasure as well as for the creation of children. Sexual intercourse is a gift from

Allah and must happen within a marriage (see Surah 25:24).

Men must not be alone with women except for their wives, in case they are tempted by them:

> Let no man be in privacy with a woman who he is not married to, or Satan will be the third.
>
> (Hadith)

Sexual activity outside of marriage is forbidden. Adultery is a serious crime:

> Nor come night to adultery: for it is a shameful (deed) and an evil, opening the road (to other evils).
>
> (Surah 17:32)

The Qur'an gives a clear punishment for adultery:

> The woman and the man guilty of adultery or fornication – flog each of them with a hundred stripes: let not compassion move you in their case, in a matter prescribed by Allah, if ye believe in Allah and the Last Day: and let a party of the Believers witness their punishment.
>
> (Surah 24:2)

Contraception

Islam teaches that Allah created the world and everything in it. Life is therefore a special gift.

For Muslims, the birth of a child is a gift of life from Allah:

> He bestows (children) male or female according to His Will (and Plan), or He bestows both males and females, and He leaves barren whom He will. For He is full of knowledge and power.
>
> (Surah 42:49–50)

This means that Muslims should submit to Allah's will about whether pregnancies happen or not.

Contraception is not welcomed. However, in 1971, the Conference on Islam and Family Planning agreed that contraception was allowed under certain circumstances:

- if there was a threat to the mother's health
- if the use of contraception would help a woman who already had children
- where there was a chance of the child being born with mental or physical deformities
- where the family did not have the money to raise a child.

Muslims prefer the use of the rhythm method of contraception. This means that intercourse takes place at the time of the month when the woman is known to be least fertile.

Discussion

Do you think that today, when people often live for more than 75 years, it is reasonable to expect that they should stay married for life? Try to support your answer with reasons.

Activity

Write a sentence about each of: *divorce, adultery, contraception.*

Judaism

Jewish marriage ceremonies

Marriage and the family are at the very centre of Jewish life. Many ceremonies of Jewish worship take place at home, so **kiddushin** (marriage) is very important. The Talmud says that:

> A man without a woman is doomed to an existence without joy, without blessing, without experiencing life's true goodness, without Torah, without protection and without peace.

Marriage comes into the first book of the Torah, Genesis:

> Therefore a man shall leave his father and mother and cling to his wife and they shall become one flesh.
>
> (Genesis 2:24)

This is explained in the Midrash:

> G-d created the first human being half male, half female. He then separated the two parts to form a man and a woman.

A Jewish wedding may take place in a synagogue or anywhere else. The important part is that the bride and groom must stand under a **huppah** (wedding canopy). This represents their new home together.

The **ketubah** is a marriage contract. The groom makes promises about how he will look after his wife. The ketubah is a very important part of the marriage ceremony. It may hang over the bed in the new couple's home.

Signing the ketubah, the marriage contract.

A Jewish wedding ceremony is very short. The man makes a vow to the woman as he gives her a ring:

> Behold, you are consecrated to me by means of this ring, according to the rituals of Moses and Israel.

After this the **Sheva Berachos** (Seven) Blessings are said over a glass of wine.

The Seven Blessings

Blessed are You, HASHEM, our G-d, King of the universe, Who has created everything for His glory.

Blessed are You, HASHEM, our G-d, King of the universe, Who fashioned the Man.

Blessed are You, HASHEM, our G-d, King of the universe, Who fashioned the Man in His image, in the image of his likeness. And prepared for him – from himself – a building for eternity. Blessed are You, HASHEM, Who fashioned the Man.

A Jewish wedding ceremony.

Bring intense joy – and exultation to the barren one – through the in-gathering of her children amidst her in gladness. Blessed are You, HASHEM, Who gladdens Zion through her children.

Gladden the beloved companions as You gladdened Your creature in the Garden of Eden from aforetime. Blessed are You, HASHEM, Who gladdens groom and bride.

Blessed are You, HASHEM, our G-d, King of the universe, Who created joy and gladness, groom and bride, mirth, glad song, pleasure, delight, love, brotherhood, peace, and companionship. HASHEM, our G-d, let there soon be heard in the cities of Judah and the streets of Jerusalem the sound of joy and the sound of gladness, the voice of the groom and the voice of the bride, the sound of the grooms' jubilance from their canopies and of youths from their song-filled feasts. Blessed are You, Who gladdens the groom with the bride.

Blessed are You HASHEM, our G-d, King of the universe, Who creates the fruit of the vine.

At the end of the ceremony the groom smashes a glass under his foot. Some people say that it shows that marriage can be easily broken. Others think that it remembers the destruction of the Jerusalem Temple in 70 CE.

The roles of men and women within a Jewish family

The family is a very important part of Judaism. When Abraham was a very old man he was promised that he would have many descendants:

> Gaze, now, towards the Heavens, and count the stars if you are able to count them!… So shall your offspring be.
>
> (Genesis 15:5)

The family is the centre of all Jewish life and worship. It is often said that the home, rather than the synagogue, is the centre of Jewish worship.

Judaism has very strict rules about the relationships between husband and wife. A married couple is complete, while men and women on their own are incomplete.

Traditionally, Jewish women have no part to play in public prayer and worship and are not allowed to study the Torah. The woman's responsibility was to look after the home and the family. In this traditional view, it is the responsibility of the man to provide for his family, to care for his wife and children and to observe his religious duties.

These traditional views are still important within Judaism but they are beginning to change. Many Jewish wives now go out to work as well as look after their family. In some Jewish traditions, women do take part in public prayer and worship.

Discussion

Do you think there are jobs in the home, or in the world of work, that are more suitable for men than for women? Give reasons to support your argument.

Activity

Write a description of a Jewish wedding. Explain the most important parts.

Glossary words

kiddushin

huppah

ketubah

Sheva Berachos

Jewish beliefs about divorce

Jews do accept that sometimes divorce is necessary. To get a divorce a man must issue his wife with a **get**, a divorce document. This is the rule which is found in the book of Deuteronomy:

> If a man marries a woman and lives with her, and it will be that she will not find favour in his eyes, for he found in her a matter of immorality, and he wrote her a bill of divorce and presented it into her hand, and sent her from his house.
>
> (Deuteronomy 24:1)

A divorce is not allowed to take place for three months, to make sure that the woman is not pregnant.

Without a get people cannot remarry. Even if a husband has left his wife, he can still refuse to divorce her. If he does refuse then the woman cannot remarry.

Progressive Jews are less traditional than Orthodox Jews. Progressive Jews may allow the woman to obtain a get if her husband refuses to divorce her.

In the past, most Jews lived close together in small communities. They mixed with other Jews and so they married other Jews. Today, many young Jews live and work outside of the Jewish community and they may meet and fall in love with someone who is not Jewish. Strict Orthodox Jews do not permit such marriages. A father who finds that his son or daughter intends to marry someone who is not Jewish may say the **Kaddish** (the prayer said at funerals), because to them their child is dead:

> You shall not intermarry with them; you shall not give your daughter to his son, and you shall not take his daughter for your son, for he will cause your child to turn away from after Me and they will worship the gods of others; then HASHEM'S wrath will burn against you and He will destroy you quickly.
>
> (Deuteronomy 7:3–4)

Jewish beliefs about sexual relationships and contraception

Jews live according to **mitzvot** (rules) found in the Torah and the Talmud (oral Torah). Sex plays a very important part in human relationships. Judaism recognises the importance of sexual desire but believes that this must be carefully controlled. Sex should take place only within a marriage.

Judaism does not believe that having children is the only purpose of sex. It says that it is a physical way in which two married people can show their love for one another.

Adultery is forbidden by the seventh commandment. This law is very important for religious Jews.

In some religions, some people show their devotion to G-d by becoming *celibate* (that is, not having sexual relationships). The idea of religious celibacy does not exist within Judaism. Jews believe that G-d wanted men and women to serve him by living together and producing a family. Jews would see it as 'abnormal' for people to live celibate lives as monks and nuns do.

Jews live by the laws of purity (**niddah**). During her period and for another week, a woman is not allowed to have sex. She then goes to a ritual bath called a **mikveh**. After the mikveh she and her husband can resume normal sexual

An ancient mikveh.

relations. This is mentioned in the Torah and the Talmud:

> You shall not approach a women in her time of unclean separation, to uncover her nakedness.
>
> (Leviticus 18:19)

> A wife returning from the mikveh is as fresh to her husband as on their wedding day.
>
> (Talmud)

Homosexuality is forbidden in Judaism:

> You shall not lie with a man as one lies with a woman, it is an abomination.
>
> (Leviticus 18:22)

Contraception

Sex in marriage is a very important part of Judaism. It is a husband's duty and a woman's right, so the question of contraception is very important too.

In Genesis it says that people should, 'Be fruitful and multiply, fill the earth…', and later:

> For thus said HASHEM, Creator of the heavens; He is the G-d, the One Who fashioned the earth and its Maker; He established it; He did not create it for emptiness; He fashioned it to be inhabited.
>
> (Isaiah 45:18)

This means religious Jews are not in favour of birth control. But birth control can be used if a married woman would be at risk if she became pregnant.

Contraception is not allowed when people are not married or simply feel that they do not want a child.

When contraceptives are used, they are usually taken by the woman so that sexual intercourse is still as natural as possible.

Discussion

Do you think that today, when people often live for more than 75 years, it is reasonable to expect that they should stay married for life? Try to support your answer with reasons.

Activity

Write a short paragraph explaining Jewish views about divorce.

Glossary words

get

Kaddish

mitzvot

niddah

mikveh

Christianity

(a) Describe Christian beliefs about the use of birth control (contraception). (8 marks)

(b) Explain how the beliefs of Christians might affect their attitudes towards divorce. (7 marks)

(c) 'People should only have sex if they are married to each other.'
Do you agree? Give reasons to support your answer, and show that you have thought about different points of view. You must refer to Christianity in your answer. (5 marks)

Hinduism

(a) Describe Hindu beliefs about the use of birth control (contraception). (8 marks)

(b) Explain how the beliefs of Hindus might affect their attitudes towards divorce. (7 marks)

(c) 'People should only have sex if they are married to each other.'
Do you agree? Give reasons to support your answer, and show that you have thought about different points of view. You must refer to Hinduism in your answer. (5 marks)

Islam

(a) Describe Muslim beliefs about the use of birth control (contraception). (8 marks)

(b) Explain how the beliefs of Muslims might affect their attitudes towards divorce. (7 marks)

(c) 'People should only have sex if they are married to each other.'
Do you agree? Give reasons to support your answer, and show that you have thought about different points of view. You must refer to Islam in your answer. (5 marks)

Judaism

(a) Describe Jewish beliefs about the use of birth control (contraception). (8 marks)

(b) Explain how the beliefs of Jews might affect their attitudes towards divorce. (7 marks)

Tips

For all four questions

In part **(a)**, you are being asked to show your knowledge of religious beliefs about birth control, or contraception. You need to be able to show what the views are, and explain them. Remember that different people who come from the same religion might not agree. For example, Roman Catholic and Protestant Christians are likely to hold different views, and so are Orthodox and Progressive Jews.

For part **(b)**, you need to be able to show your understanding. Try to say something about what marriage means for religious people, and how this affects their views about divorce. Again, there might be different opinions within the religion. You could explain what these are. Try to show how the beliefs might be used in everyday life. What might a religious believer in an unhappy marriage think about divorce? Why might he or she think in this way?

In part **(c)**, you need to show that you have thought about whether sex outside marriage is right or wrong. Remember that you need to refer to the religion you are studying, as well as giving your own view. You should try to support the views you give with reasons, and show that you understand how people who disagree with you might feel.

(c) 'People should only have sex if they are married to each other.'
Do you agree? Give reasons to support your answer, and show that you have thought about different points of view. You must refer to Judaism in your answer. (5 marks)

UNIT 7

Religion and Medical Ethics

Introduction

Medical ethics is about what is right and wrong in health care. Often it is about life and death. Should people be kept alive, even if they are very disabled or in great pain? Should babies be born even if no-one wants them, or if they will have serious health problems? Does everyone have the right to have a child, with the help of doctors if it is needed? Medical staff have to deal with this sort of problem every day.

Many religious people have strong beliefs about medical ethics. Most religions teach that life comes from God and is 'sacred' or holy. When people are talking about the way in which human life is special to God, they often use the phrase the **sanctity of life**.

Fertility treatment

Fertility treatment is the name for medical treatments that are tried when people want to have babies, but need medical help. There are lots of reasons why some people cannot have children naturally. Sometimes the man does not produce healthy sperm, or sometimes the woman does not produce eggs. If people very much want to have their own children, infertility can be very upsetting.

IVF

There are different kinds of fertility treatment. They do not always work, but when couples do manage to have babies, it can make them very happy. One of the most common treatments is called IVF. This stands for **in vitro fertilisation** (*in vitro* means 'in glass'). A human egg and some healthy sperm are brought together in a test tube, by doctors. If the treatment works, embryos are formed and then carefully placed inside the woman's uterus, where they can continue to develop until it is time for the baby to be born. Often, to make sure that at least one of the embryos survives, more than one egg will be fertilised. This can create 'spare' embryos. Religious people, and some others with no religious beliefs, are often worried about what happens to these spare embryos which are not used. Do they count as 'people', or as 'human life', and would it be murder to throw them away if they are not needed?

Donor sperm or eggs

Another problem can be if one of the partners in the couple cannot produce healthy sperm or eggs at all. Is it all right to use 'donor' sperm or eggs, from someone who is unknown to the couple, or does this go against the idea of a man and woman being faithful to each other?

Abortion

An abortion is when a foetus leaves the mother's uterus before it is ready to be born. When this happens naturally, which it often does, it is called a 'miscarriage'. But usually, when people talk about abortion, they are referring to 'procured abortion'. This is when someone chooses to end a pregnancy.

There are many reasons why a woman might want an abortion. She might be very young, or have become pregnant by accident, or have been raped. She might have wanted the pregnancy at first, but then things might have changed.

Medical staff often have to make important decisions about life and death.

For example, her partner might have lost his job or left her. Or medical tests might show that the baby is not growing properly and will be disabled in some way when it is born.

Having an abortion is hardly ever an easy choice to make. Two doctors have to agree that the woman would suffer unless she has an abortion. She has to make her choice as early in the pregnancy as she can. Abortion is only legal in the first 24 weeks of the pregnancy. After 28 weeks of development, the foetus is considered 'viable', which means it could live outside the womb if it was born.

Many people believe that abortion is the same as murder. They think that a foetus is a human life. Others believe that a woman should not have to go through pregnancy and birth if this is not what she wants.

Suicide

A suicide is when someone ends his or her own life. Sometimes it is called 'self-murder'. In the past suicide was treated as a crime. Today, most people think that if someone wants to commit suicide, this is often because they are very depressed. They need care, not punishment.

Euthanasia

Euthanasia is when someone is 'helped' to die, without pain, before they would have died naturally. It is different from suicide, because it is for people who cannot take their own life, because they are too ill or too disabled.

Some people think that euthanasia is the right choice for them, because they are in a lot of pain and need other people to do everything for them. Sometimes, they are very brain-damaged or have become very confused, and they cannot decide for themselves. If someone asks for euthanasia, it is called **voluntary euthanasia**. If the person has not been asked or is not able to ask, then it is called **involuntary euthanasia**. Someone else decides whether that person's life is so bad that it would be better if they were dead.

121

When someone does something that helps a patient to die, this is known as **active euthanasia**. This is against the law.

Passive euthanasia is not against the law. In cases of passive euthanasia, nothing is done on purpose to make death come more quickly, but nothing is done to keep the person alive. For example, doctors, patients, nurses and family might decide that it is better not to keep on giving food and medicine.

Some people think that euthanasia ought to be possible for those who want it. They say that it is unkind to let dying people suffer, if you could help them die with less pain. They say that we would do the same for a pet who was suffering. We would allow an animal to be 'put down' because this is the kindest thing to do. But many religious people, and others, think that euthanasia is a form of murder. They say that only God should decide how people die.

Animal research

Animals are often used in experiments. People are more aware of this fact today, and some try not to buy products that have been tested on animals.

Testing on animals is important for medicine. Most doctors say that without animal testing, we would not have the safe medicines that we need. Animal experiments were used to discover vitamins, to learn how babies grow before they are born, and to help with painkillers, prevention of polio, and treatments for asthma and diabetes. These are just a few examples. Today, scientists use experiments on animals to try and find ways of curing illnesses such as cancer.

However, some people believe that it is wrong to use animals in this way. Many of the tests are painful for the animals. Some people say that an animal has just as much right to life as a human. They say that scientists should find other ways of testing drugs which do not involve the use of animals.

Many people prefer to buy cosmetics and other products that have not been tested on animals.

Discussion

Would you be prepared to use new medicines that had not been tested on other animals first?

Activity

Explain what is meant by:

(a) *abortion*

(b) *euthanasia*

(c) *suicide*

(d) *sanctity of life*

(e) *animal research.*

Glossary words

medical ethics

sanctity of life

in vitro fertilisation

euthanasia:
    voluntary/involuntary
    active/passive

Abortion

There are many different Christian views on abortion. In the past, Christians believed that there was a time in a pregnancy when the foetus was given a soul. They thought that abortion was wrong after the soul had been given, but if it happened early enough it was allowed.

Today, the Roman Catholic Church is the only Christian church to give rules about abortion. The Roman Catholic Church says abortion is never allowed, even if the pregnancy is because of rape or the pregnant woman is very young. Abortion is only allowed if it is needed to save the life of the mother. Roman Catholics believe that the developing foetus is a person, just like a person who has been born. They believe that its life is sacred, and it would be murder to kill it.

Other Christians from different churches might agree with this view, and believe that abortion is always wrong. Sometimes the Bible is used to support this view. For example, in the Old Testament, Jeremiah the prophet is told by God:

> Before I formed you in the womb, I knew you, and before you were born I consecrated you: I appointed you a prophet to the nations.
>
> (Jeremiah 1:5)

This verse seems to say that God has a plan for each person. Abortion might be seen as a way of spoiling the plans that God has made for people.

But the other Christian churches teach that abortion has to be a personal choice. Sometimes, a woman or a couple might want to end a pregnancy if the baby will be born disabled. They might think it is best if the mother is very young, or has not got much money, or just does not want a baby. Some Christians believe that the most important Bible teaching to use is the Golden Rule:

> In everything do to others as you would have them do to you.
>
> (Matthew 7:12)

This means that Christians should try to treat other people in the way they would like to be treated themselves. If they think that they might want an abortion one day, then they should let other people have them, too.

They might try to put into practice the Christian principle of **agape** (unconditional love). This means trying to work out what is the most loving thing to do. They might think that sometimes abortion could be the kindest answer to the problem.

Fertility treatment

The Bible does not teach about fertility treatment, because fertility treatment was invented after the Bible was written. In the Bible, if someone could not have children, people thought that was God's plan for them:

> Hannah had no children ... because the Lord had closed her womb.
>
> (1 Samuel 1:2,6)

Not all Christians agree about fertility treatment. Some Christians believe that people who want babies should be given medical help if they need it, because it will make them happy. They think that giving fertility treatment is the most loving way to behave. It could start a new human life, which is a good thing.

But other Christians are not sure about fertility treatment. They might say that if people have no children, this is God's way of saying that he has different plans for

Fertility treatment, when it works, gives people the chance to enjoy all the benefits of being parents.

them. Some kinds of fertility treatment leave 'spare' embryos, and some Christians think these should be treated as human lives. Some Christians think it is wrong to use eggs or sperm from a donor, and not from the husband or wife. Roman Catholics often disagree with fertility treatment.

Discussion

Do you think there should be rules about who should and should not be allowed to have fertility treatment? For example, should women over 50, or gay couples, or disabled people, be helped to have babies if they are not able to conceive naturally?

Activity

1 Explain why Christians might have different views about abortion.

2 What is your own view about fertility treatment? Give reasons for your answer.

Glossary words

agape

Euthanasia and suicide

Christians believe all human life is sacred. Each person is known by God, who plans their life and decides how long they should live:

> In your book were written all the days that were formed for me, when none of them as yet existed.
>
> (Psalm 139:16)

Because of this, many Christians think that euthanasia and suicide are wrong. They believe that God gave the gift of life, so people should not choose when to take it away. They say it shows no faith in God. Christians should trust God to know when it is the right time for them to die. God will always know what is best.

Christians often say that there is a difference between killing someone (**active euthanasia**) and letting them die instead of keeping their lives going (**passive euthanasia**). For many Christians, killing another person is always wrong. It is wrong even when the person doing the killing is trying to be kind and save someone from suffering. But letting someone die is different. There is a time when we have to die, and we should try to understand that, not try to keep people alive for as long as possible.

Christians agree that killing is wrong, but they also say that no-one has to try and keep a life going on and on for ever. Doctors are allowed to decide to stop treatment, but they are not allowed to kill.

Double effect

The Roman Catholic Church teaches a rule known as the law of **double effect**. This rule says euthanasia is only allowed if it happens because of treatment that is meant to help. For example, a patient dying in a lot of pain might need a strong painkiller. 'Double effect' says that they can have the painkiller, even if it makes death come more quickly.

Palliative care

Many Christians believe that a **hospice** can give dying people the care they need. Hospices do not use euthanasia, but instead they give special care to help make a dying patient as comfortable as possible (this is called **palliative care**). They help the patient and the family and friends to come to terms with death. They help to sort out money problems or any other worries. Then when death comes, it is peaceful and as painless as possible.

Most Christians also understand that people commit suicide only when they are very unhappy. Some Christians volunteer to help with groups such as The Samaritans, which are always there to talk to people who are very unhappy.

The use of animals in medical research

Christians believe that humans are the most important thing God made. They think other animals were made for people to control and to rule. The Bible teaches:

> God blessed them, and God said to them, Be fruitful and multiply, and fill the earth and subdue it; and have dominion over the fish of the sea and over the birds of the air and over every living thing that moves upon the earth.
>
> (Genesis 1:28)

Animals are not believed to have a 'soul'. Most Christians are happy to eat meat and to keep animals as pets or in zoos. Many Christians now think that animals deserve respect because they were made by God. They think it is wrong to be cruel to animals.

But most of the Christian churches agree that sometimes animals should be used for medical research. The Church of England says that animal research can be used to help understanding of medicine. The Roman Catholic Church agrees, and says that it is all right to use animals for

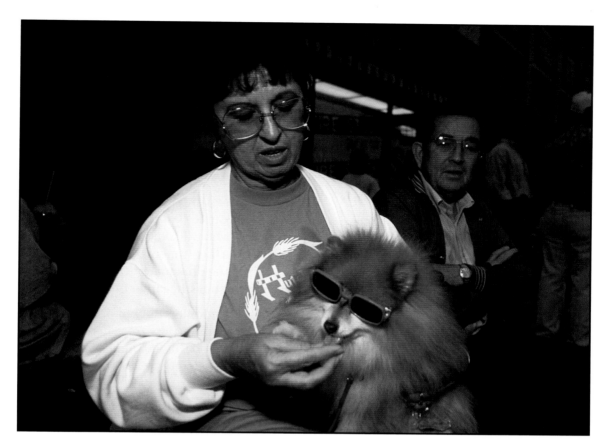

Roman Catholics believe that it is wrong to make too much fuss of pets while doing nothing about the starving people of the world.

food and clothing. It teaches that people should not spoil their animals with silly things that cost a lot of money, when there are humans who are suffering in the world. They believe that it is wrong to spend a lot of money on the best dog foods when there are people who are starving in the world.

So most Christians think that animal research for medicine is important, but that people should not be cruel to animals.

Discussion

Christians believe that humans are more important than other animals. What do you think about this?

Activity

1 Explain why most Christians believe that euthanasia is wrong.

2 How might Christians help someone who is depressed, so that they don't commit suicide?

Glossary words

active euthanasia

passive euthanasia

double effect

hospice

palliative care

Abortion

Many Hindus believe that abortion and contraception (birth control) are wrong. They think that marrying and having children is a duty for every adult. Many Hindu holy books say that abortion is a crime. It goes against Hindu teaching about **ahimsa** (non-violence) because it does not respect the life of the growing foetus. It stops the soul (**Atman**) living in the foetus from being reborn into a new life. Hindus believe that all life is holy, and that it brings bad **karma** if a person decides to end a pregnancy.

But abortion does happen among Hindus. Most Hindus in India think abortion should not be against the law. Many believe that abortion is better than having a baby in a family where it is not wanted and there is not enough money. Some Hindus might also choose abortion if the foetus is not growing normally, or if there is a risk to the health of the mother, or if the woman has been raped.

Hindu couples have always wanted sons rather than daughters. Daughters are still seen as a problem, because their parents have to find money for them when they marry (a dowry). A son is much more likely to be able to earn his own living and to support his parents in their old age. Doctors can now tell if a baby is going to be a girl or a boy, before it is born. Sometimes, Hindu couples who already have daughters, or who want only one child, might choose abortion if the baby will be a girl.

Fertility treatment

Fertility is an important part of Hinduism. Married couples are keen to have at least one son, who will look after his parents and make sure their funeral is done properly. It is part of the **dharma**, or right way of life, for a man to be the father of sons.

If a Hindu couple want children but it is difficult, then fertility treatment is often seen as a good thing. Hindus do not like methods of fertility treatment that need sperm or eggs from another person outside the marriage. This is because they want the baby to carry on the same genes as its father, and they also want the baby to be from the same social group (**varna**). Some Hindus also do not like methods of fertility treatment that leave 'spare' embryos. But most Hindus think that fertility treatment is a good thing, because it helps them to have children and they think this is very important.

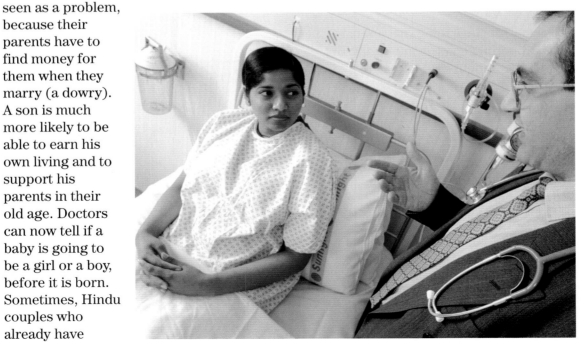

In India, the government is trying to stop women having an abortion just because the expected baby is a girl.

In many parts of India, fertility treatment is not a possibility. It is something that is only for rich people. People who are poor and cannot have children of their own sometimes adopt a child, maybe from relations who have many children and cannot afford to look after all of them. This is often seen as a good answer to the problem.

Discussion

Do you think parents should be allowed to choose the sex of their children? What do you think most people would choose?

Activity

Explain in your own words what a Hindu might think about (a) abortion and (b) fertility treatment.

Glossary words

ahimsa

Atman

karma

dharma

varna

Euthanasia and suicide

Euthanasia

Because Hindus believe that all of life is sacred, they disagree with euthanasia. One of the most important ideas in Hinduism is ahimsa, or harmlessness. They believe it is always wrong to take life, even when someone else is ill or in pain. If someone is suffering, this is believed to be the result of karma. The person is suffering because they have done wrong things in the past, either in this life or in a past life. If they die too soon there will still be some bad karma left for the person's next life. People who are caring for dying patients should do all they can to look after them, but they should not end the patient's life.

Sometimes a Hindu who is very old or very ill decides that the right time has come for death, and stops eating and drinking to make it happen. This way of bringing death more quickly is often admired as a sign of great holiness. It is not the same as euthanasia, because it does not involve anyone apart from the person who wishes to die; no-one else is asked to help with the death, or to make any decisions about it.

Suicide

Suicide is wrong in Hinduism, when it is because of hopelessness and depression. But when Hindus kill themselves because they want to make a sacrifice for others, or because they do not want to be parted from someone who has just died, this is accepted, and is often seen as a good thing. **Suttee** or **sati** is an example of this kind of suicide. It is the name of an old custom in which a Hindu widow would throw herself on the flames of her husband's funeral fire, as a way of showing her love. People once believed that this death would earn the woman great karma and good luck in the next life. The custom is now against the law in India.

The use of animals in medical research

Hindus respect all living things. They do not believe that people are more important than other kinds of animals. Some animals are often used in Hindu images of the gods. For example, the bull is often seen with the god Shiva, the tiger with the goddess Durga, the monkey with Hanuman and the elephant with Ganesha. The cow is very important in Hinduism, as a holy animal (see page 34). Animals are treated with great care and respect, and many Hindus will not eat meat because of their respect for animals.

The Hindu principle of ahimsa (see page 34) involves doing no harm to other living creatures. Hurting or destroying

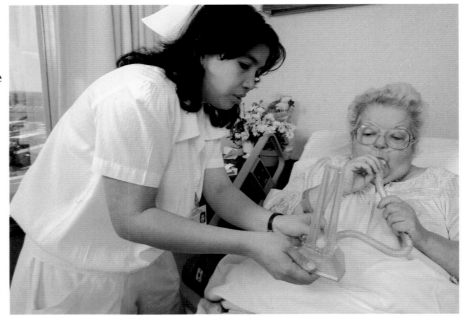

Hindus believe that everything should be done to make ill people more comfortable, but this should not involve the taking of a life.

animal life leads to bad karma. It will bring bad luck in the next life.

For all of these reasons, Hindus do not agree with cruelty to animals. But some Hindus think that animals could be used in medical research if there is no other way of doing the tests.

Discussion

What do you think about the Hindu idea that people are not much more important than any other animals?

Activity

1 Explain in your own words what Hindus think about euthanasia.

2 Do you think that humans have the right to use other animals for food and in medical experiments? Give reasons for your answer.

Glossary words

suttee/sati

Abortion

Islam does not allow abortion in almost any circumstances. It is seen as a crime against a living human being.

However, an abortion can take place if a doctor says that the pregnancy would kill the mother. The abortion should take place as early as possible so that the foetus has not developed. For the first four months the mother's rights are greater than those of the child. After this time they have equal rights.

Imam Al-Ghazzali (born 1058, died 1111) said:

> Contraception is not like abortion. Abortion is a crime against an existing being. Existence has various stages. The first is the settling of the semen in the womb and its mixing with the secretions [egg] of the woman. It is then ready to receive life. Disturbing it is a crime. When it develops further and becomes a lump, abortion is a greater crime. When it acquires a soul and its creation is complete the crime becomes even more grievous. The crime reaches its maximum seriousness after the foetus is separated from its mother alive.

If a pregnant woman is guilty of a crime and sentenced to death, she cannot be executed until after the baby is born.

Muslims have different views about when a foetus becomes a person. Some experts believe that the foetus has a soul after 42 days. Others say it only has a soul after 120 days from conception.

Fertility treatment

Having children is a very important part of a Muslim marriage. It is very difficult when a couple find that they cannot have children.

Muslims look at the women in the Qur'an and in the life of Muhammad ﷺ for ways of coping with this. Sara, the wife of Ibrahim, had no children until she was 90. Then her future pregnancy was announced by angels:

> They said, 'Fear not,' and they gave him glad tidings of a son endowed with knowledge. But his wife came forward (laughing) aloud: she smote her forehead and said: 'A barren old woman!' They said, 'Even so has thy Lord spoken: and He is full of Wisdom and Knowledge.'
>
> (Surah 51:28–30)

Zakariya prays to the Lord for a child and his elderly wife Ishba gives birth to a child, Yabya:

> And (remember) Zakariya, when he cried to his Lord: 'O my Lord! leave me not without offspring, though Thou art the best of inheritors.' So We listened to him: and We granted him Yabya: we cured his wife's (barrenness) for him. These (three) were ever quick in emulation in good works; they used to call on Us with love and reverence, and humble themselves before Us.
>
> (Surah 21:89–90)

Women who cannot have children might say that although Sara and Ishba were very old, they still had children eventually.

Muhammad ﷺ had children with his first wife Khadijah, but not with any of his other wives: Sawda, Aisha, Hafsa, Umm Salamah, Zaynab bint Jahshm Juwayriyya, Rayhana, Umm Habiba, Safiyya, and Maymuna.

The idea of a man having more than one wife is sometimes suggested as a way around a fertility problem but this is not common and still does help the woman who wants children.

Children are a very important part of a Muslim marriage.

Some Muslims believe that people should accept Allah's will if they cannot have children. Others see infertility as a disease and say that Muslims should look for a treament.

IVF is one possibility. Although some of the fertilised eggs die, this is not seen as a problem. Muslims say that these embryos are not human beings. These 'spare' embryos could be used for stem cell research to cure other conditions. However, it would not be lawful to donate embryos to another woman. This would mean a baby being born to parents who are not married.

Discussion

Do you think a woman has a right to have a child, or should she see it as a gift from God?

Activity

Write a sentence about Muslim views on (a) abortion and (b) fertility treatment.

Euthanasia and suicide

Muslims are against euthanasia and suicide. Allah tests people with suffering. If people keep their faith through these tests, Allah rewards them:

> O ye who believe! Seek help with patient Perseverance and Prayer: for Allah is with those who patiently persevere ... Be sure we shall test you with something of fear and hunger, some loss in goods or lives or the fruits (of your toil), but give glad tidings to those who patiently persevere – who say, when afflicted with calamity: 'To Allah we belong, and to Him is our return.'
>
> (Surah 2:153–156)

Every soul is created by Allah, so every life is sacred:

> Nor kill (or destroy) yourselves: for verily Allah hath been to you most Merciful!
>
> (Surah 4:29)

If people suffer it is to test their **iman** (faith). Nothing that happens to a person is a good enough reason to end life. The Prophet Muhammad ﷺ said that anyone who killed themselves would go to hell:

> Anyone who throws themselves down from a rock and commits suicide will be throwing themselves into Hell. A person who drinks poison and kills themselves will drink it for ever in Hell. A person who stabs themselves will stab themselves for ever in Hell.
>
> (Hadith)

Only Allah can decide when someone dies:

> When their Term expires, they would not be able to delay (the punishment) for a single hour, just as they would not be able to anticipate it (for a single hour).
>
> (Surah 16:61)

> Nor can a soul die except by Allah's leave, the term being fixed as by writing.
>
> (Surah 3:145)

If someone does commit suicide it shows that the **ummah** (Muslim community) has failed to take care of the person.

Euthanasia is not allowed in Islam. It is **zalim** – doing something wrong against Allah, other people, or yourself. Everyone must try to protect life. Suffering is not seen as a good thing and everything possible should be done to ease pain but the person must be kept alive.

The use of animals in medical research

All life, animal and human, belongs to Allah:

> He has created man from a sperm-drop and behold this same (man) becomes an open disputer! And cattle He has created for you (men): from them ye derive warmth, and numerous benefits, and of their (meat) ye eat. And ye have a sense of pride and beauty in them as ye drive them back home in the evening, and as ye lead them forth to pasture in the morning. And they carry your heavy loads to lands that you could not (otherwise) reach except with souls distressed: for your Lord is indeed Most Kind, Most Merciful.
>
> (Surah 16:4–7)

> There is not an animal (that lives) on the earth, nor a being that flies on its wings, but (forms part of) communities like you. Nothing have we omitted from the Book, and they (all) shall be gathered to their Lord in the end.
>
> (Surah 6:38)

Muslims believe that humans have a duty towards all living beings. However, humans are more important than animals. Experiments on animals can be done to help human life but animals are an important part of Allah's creation:

> Seest thou not that it is Allah Whose praises all beings in the heavens and on earth do celebrate, and the birds (of the

Humans have a duty to all living creatures.

air) with wings outspread? Each one knows its own (mode of) prayer and praise. And Allah knows well all that they do.

(Surah 24:42)

Muhammad ﷺ showed respect to animals. One story says that Muhammad ﷺ saw an army of ants heading towards a fire, so he ordered the fire to be put out so that the ants would not be harmed. Again when Muhammad ﷺ was travelling from Makkah to al-Madinah and hid from his enemies in a cave, a spider spun a web across the entrance and a dove nested on a ledge outside in order to protect him.

In the 13th century a Muslim lawyer called Izz ad-Din ibn Abd as-Salam gave legal rights to animals based on Shari'ah (Muslim law).

At the World Wide Fund for Nature International in 1986, the Muslim representative, Dr Abdullah Omar Nasseef, stressed that humans had a responsibility to look after the earth and the animals:

> God created mankind – a very special creation because mankind alone was created with reason and the power to think and even the means to turn against his Creator ... mankind's role on earth is that of a khalifa, a viceregent or trustee of God. We are God's stewards and agents on Earth. We are not masters of this Earth; it does not belong to us to do what we wish. It belongs to God and He has entrusted us with its safekeeping ... His trustees are responsible for maintaining the unity of His creation, the integrity of the Earth, its flora and fauna, its wildlife and natural environment.

Discussion

Do you think there are any times when religious people might say that someone was right to commit suicide?

Activity

1 Explain how a Muslim doctor might treat a patient who was dying in great pain.

2 What might a Muslim say to someone who was thinking of committing suicide?

Glossary words

iman

ummah

zalim

Abortion

G-d created human beings, so G-d is in charge of when they live and when they die. Jews say that abortion goes against G-d's plan for the world and destroys a potential human being. However, the life of a human being is thought to be more important than the life of an unborn child.

> If men shall fight and they collide with a pregnant woman and she miscarries, but there will be no fatality, he shall surely be punished as the husband of the woman shall cause to be assessed against him, and he shall pay it by order of judges. But if there shall be fatality, then you shall award a life for a life; an eye for an eye, a tooth for a tooth, a hand for a hand, a foot for a foot; a burn for a burn, a wound for a wound, a bruise for a bruise.
>
> (Exodus 21:23–25)

This passage is often misunderstood. It does not mean that someone should take a hand if they have lost a hand. It means that there is a limit to what people can take. Money should be paid equal to the value of what is lost.

Jews believe that a foetus becomes a person at the moment of birth, not at conception. So abortion is not murder.

> If a woman is in difficult labour (to the point that her life may be in danger) her child must be cut up while it is still in her womb since the life of the mother is more important than the life of the foetus. But if the greater part of the child has already emerged it may not be damaged, since one life cannot be more important than another.
>
> (Mishnah)

The life and well-being of the mother is the most important part of this argument and abortion is allowed if the mother or child is at risk or if the pregnancy is the result of rape. It is the mother's decision.

Fertility treatment

There is no teaching in the Bible about fertility treatment. In the past, if people had no children, then they were often very unhappy, but there was nothing they could do about it. In the Bible it was believed to be G-d's decision:

> Hannah had no children ... for HASHEM had closed her womb.
>
> (1 Samuel 1:2,6)

Judaism sees children as a blessing to a family and as a commandment. This means that G-d wishes married people to do all they can to have children:

> Whoever adds even one Jewish soul is considered as having created an (entire) world.
>
> (Maimonides)

Some Jews believe that if a woman cannot become pregnant in the normal way, other means can be used. Fertility treatment is allowed, even if the sperm comes from a donor. The baby is still seen as legitimate (born within the marriage), even though the sperm came from another man.

Discussion

Does a woman have a right to have a child? Or should she see it as a gift from G-d?

Activity

Explain what Jews believe about abortion.

Euthanasia and suicide

In Judaism, all human life is sacred. People were G-d's special creation, and G-d knows everyone and plans their lives:

> your eyes saw my unformed body.
> All the days ordained for me
> were written in your book
> before one of them came to be.
>
> (Psalm 139:16)

Because life is sacred, suicide is a sin. 'One who intentionally takes one's life has no share in the world to come.' People who commit suicide are not given a normal funeral service and are not buried near other Jews.

There are people in the Torah who took their own life. Samson pulls down the columns of the temple, killing himself and his enemies. Saul falls on his sword and dies rather than being captured alive by the Philistines and to protect his soldiers. In cases like these, suicide is allowed because of the noble reasons behind it.

Judaism does not agree with euthanasia because only G-d can decide when a person should die.

According to the Talmud, someone who shoots a man as he falls off a cliff to certain death is still guilty of murder. This is because the man has died too soon, before G-d had decided he should.

However, the words of Rabbi Moses Isserles are used to argue that life-support machines should be turned off if there is no hope of the patient's recovery:

> If there is anything that causes a hindrance to the departure of the soul ... then it is permissible to remove it.

Life-support machines keep people alive who would otherwise die. This means they do 'cause a hindrance' (put an obstacle in the way) to the person who is dying.

The use of animals in medical research

G-d said:

> Let us make Man in Our image, after Our likeness. They shall rule over the fish of the sea, the birds of the sky, and over the animals, the whole earth, and every creeping thing that creeps upon the earth.
>
> (Genesis 1:26)

> G-d said, 'Behold, I have given to you all the herbage yielding seed that is on the surface of the entire earth, and every tree that has seed-yielding fruit; it shall be yours for food.'
>
> (Genesis 1:29)

These two passages show that G-d gave humans power over animals and all life on earth. Does this mean that humans have the right to do what they like with animals?

In the Jewish scriptures animals were given as sacrifices to G-d in the Temple in Jerusalem. In some ways, though, this was a kind of respect to animals. People sacrificed the most valuable things they had.

Samson pulling down the columns of the temple.

It is clear that the early Jews were concerned about their animals. Adam gave all living creatures their names:

> Now, HASHEM G-d had formed out of the ground every beast of the field and every bird of the sky, and brought them to the man to see what he would call each one; and whatever the man called each living creature, that remained its name. And the man assigned names to all the cattle and to the birds of the sky and to every beast of the field...
>
> (Genesis 2:19–20)

That animals are to be shown respect is shown in several passages:

> You shall not muzzle an ox in its threshing.
>
> (Deuteronomy 25:4)

> The righteous one knows [the needs of] his animal's soul...
>
> (Proverbs 12:10)

Animals are also mentioned in the Ten Commandments:

> Safeguard the Sabbath day to sanctify it, as HASHEM, your G-d, has commanded you. Six days shall you labour and accomplish all your work; but the seventh day is Sabbath to HASHEM, your G-d; you shall not do any work – you, your son, your daughter, your slave, your maidservant, your ox, your donkey, and your every animal, and your convert within your gates, in order that your slave and your maidservant may rest like you.
>
> (Deuteronomy 5:12–14)

Here animals are to be given a day's rest, just like humans.

At the 1986 meeting of the World Wide Fund for Nature International held at Assisi, Rabbi Arthur Hertzberg said that:

> ...when the whole world is in peril, when the environment is in danger of being poisoned and various species, both plant and animal are becoming extinct. It is our Jewish responsibility to put the defence of the whole of nature at the very centre of our concern.

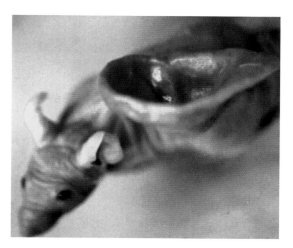

Although animals are to be respected and treated without cruelty, they are not as important as humans. They were created to be useful to humans. This means that for most Jews, animals can be used for scientific experiments as long as the experiments are necessary and the animals suffer as little as possible.

Judaism does allow the use of animals for organ transplants. Even pigs, which are usually thought to be unclean, can be used in this way.

Discussion

Are there any times when religious people might say that someone was right to commit suicide?

Activity

1 What do Jews believe about euthanasia and suicide?

2 What do Jews think about the use of animals in medical research?

Practice GCSE questions

Christianity

(a) Describe Christian beliefs about abortion.

(8 marks)

(b) Explain how having Christian beliefs might affect someone who was dying from a painful illness and considering euthanasia.

(7 marks)

(c) 'Medicines should not be given to people unless they have first been tested on animals.' Do you agree? Give reasons to support your answer and show that you have thought about different points of view. You must refer to Christianity in your answer. (5 marks)

Hinduism

(a) Describe Hindu beliefs about abortion.

(8 marks)

(b) Explain how having Hindu beliefs might affect someone who was dying from a painful illness and considering euthanasia. (7 marks)

(c) 'Medicines should not be given to people unless they have first been tested on animals.' Do you agree? Give reasons to support your answer and show that you have thought about different points of view. You must refer to Hinduism in your answer. (5 marks)

Islam

(a) Describe Muslim beliefs about abortion.

(8 marks)

(b) Explain how having Muslim beliefs might affect someone who was dying from a painful illness and considering euthanasia. (7 marks)

(c) 'Medicines should not be given to people unless they have first been tested on animals.' Do you agree? Give reasons to support your answer and show that you have thought about different points of view. You must refer to Islam in your answer. (5 marks)

Tips

For all four questions

Remember that in part **(a)**, you are being asked to describe the beliefs of members of the religion you are studying. You do not need to give your own view, but should just describe the beliefs you have been learning about. You might be able to refer to the holy books of the religion, or say something about what it means to believe in the 'sanctity of life' (life as sacred because God created it).

In part **(b)**, you need to think about how religious beliefs might affect someone who had to decide if euthanasia is right or wrong. You have to try to think about how a religious person would feel, and the reasons they might give.

In part **(c)**, you need to give your own view, and compare your opinions with those of members of the religion you are studying. What do religious believers think about the use of animals for medical research? Does this agree with your own view? Remember to explain different opinions, and to support the different views with reasons.

Judaism

(a) Describe Jewish beliefs about abortion.

(8 marks)

(b) Explain how having Jewish beliefs might affect someone who was dying from a painful illness and considering euthanasia. (7 marks)

(c) 'Medicines should not be given to people unless they have first been tested on animals.' Do you agree? Give reasons to support your answer and show that you have thought about different points of view. You must refer to Judaism in your answer. (5 marks)

UNIT 8
Religion and Equality

Christianity

Biblical teaching about equality

The Bible teaches that all people matter to God. Everyone is made 'in the image of God' (Genesis 1:27). The book of the Acts of the Apostles says that God does not have favourites:

> Then Peter began to speak: 'I now realise how true it is that God does not show favouritism but accepts men from every nation who fear him and do what is right.'
>
> (Acts 10:34)

Christians believe that God loves all people. It does not matter if they are men or women, black or white, rich or poor, or what they look like. Christians believe that people should care for each other in the same way. In the letter to the Galatians, Paul teaches people that they should understand that everybody is important:

> There is neither Jew nor Greek, slave nor free, male nor female, for you are all one in Christ Jesus.
>
> (Galatians 3:28)

Christian attitudes towards racism

There are Christians of all different colours and nationalities. Christians believe all people are made by God and loved by God equally.

Racism is the belief that some people are better than others because of the colour of their skin or their ethnic origin. Christianity teaches that racism can never be right.

Once a man asked Jesus which people he should treat as his neighbours, and which

people were not important. Jesus answered by telling the parable of the Good Samaritan. At the time of Jesus, the Jews did not like the Samaritans, who were a different race. No-one wanted to mix with them. The parable of the Good Samaritan teaches that people should treat each other as neighbours and look after them. Race should not matter.

Christians have not always set a good example against racism. Some Christians in the past have been slave-owners or have supported racist ideas. But there have also been many Christians who have given their lives to fight racism, because they believed that helping to get rid of racism is an important way of putting Christian beliefs into practice.

Martin Luther King was a Christian who lived in America at a time when black people and white people were often kept apart (**segregation**). Black people were not allowed to use the same schools, restaurants or swimming pools as white people. They were not allowed to sit down on buses if a white person wanted the seat. Martin Luther King was black. His Christian beliefs led him to work against racism. He was a very powerful speaker. Hundreds of people came to hear him and to join in the protests. His belief in God helped him to carry on, even when people made threats against his life. It is now against the law in America to treat people badly because of their race. Martin Luther King was shot dead when he was 39.

Trevor Huddleston and **Desmond Tutu** worked in South Africa to try and break down **apartheid**. In South Africa, there used to be laws that made black

Desmond Tutu is a Christian who puts his beliefs into action by campaigning against racial discrimination.

people live in poor areas with very few rights, while the white people owned big houses and factories and mines. Black people often had to live in hostels, away from their families, so that they could get work. Trevor Huddleston and Desmond Tutu both put Christian beliefs into action by working to end apartheid. They told the rest of the world what was happening, and got other countries to stop trading with South Africa until it changed its laws.

The role of women in Christian society

Some Christians believe that men and women have different skills and should do different things. Men have stronger bodies. Women can become pregnant and breastfeed their children. Some Christians say that God made men and women different because they are meant to do different things with their lives. Men should do the hard work, and make money for their families. Women should take care of the children and the home.

Parts of the Bible agree with this view of different roles for men and women.

Other Christians do not agree. They believe that God made men and women to be equal. They say women and men should share childcare, if they are parents. They should both have equal choice about whether or not to go out to work.

Many Christians believe that only men should become priests, not women. They say only a man should be able to say the words of Jesus at the Last Supper. Other Christian churches have always had women leaders as well as men.

Discussion

Do you think men and women should have exactly the same chances, or do you think they should recognise their different skills? Give reasons for your answer.

Activity

1 Explain why Christians believe that racial prejudice is wrong.

2 Read the Parable of the Good Samaritan, in Luke 10. Write the story in your own words.

3 Choose *either* Martin Luther King *or* Trevor Huddleston *or* Desmond Tutu, and find out more about their work to fight racism. Write two or three paragraphs about how they put their Christian beliefs into practice.

Glossary words

segregation

apartheid

Christian attitudes towards other world religions

Some people believe that Christianity is the only true religion. They think that all other religions are false. This belief is based on a passage from John's gospel:

> Jesus answered, 'I am the way and the truth and the life. No-one comes to the Father except through me.'
>
> (John 14:6)

Some Christians think that this means heaven is only for Christian believers. They say that there would be no point in Jesus dying and rising again if there were already lots of other ways to reach God. Some Christians go to other parts of the world as missionaries. They tell other people about being a Christian, and hope that they will become Christians too.

Christianity is an **evangelical** religion. This means that Christians think other people should be told about Christianity. Some Christians talk about their faith in the street, visit people in their homes or give out leaflets to help other people to find out more about Christianity.

Other Christians, however, hold different views. They believe that everyone who is trying to follow God is doing the right thing, even if they come from a different religion. They want people from different religions to worship God together, and try to understand each other better. They think that God will be pleased with all religious people, not just Christians.

Christians often disagree with each other. One group of Christians might think another group has wrong beliefs, or does not worship God in the right way. They might disagree about having women priests, or about who is head of the church. Some Christians try hard to stop these arguments. They work to help different Christian groups live together in peace. This kind of work is known as the **ecumenical movement**.

Christian beliefs about forgiveness and reconciliation

Christianity teaches that people should not keep remembering their differences for years. They should try to copy the forgiveness of God. The Lord's Prayer, taught by Jesus and used every day by Christians around the world, reminds people that they should be forgiving if they expect God to forgive them:

> Our Father, who art in heaven
> Hallowed be thy name.
> Thy kingdom come, thy will be done
> on earth as it is in heaven.
> Give us this day our daily bread, and
> forgive us our trespasses, as we forgive
> those who trespass against us.
> And lead us not into temptation,
> but deliver us from evil.
> For thine is the kingdom, the power and
> the glory, for ever and ever, Amen.

Some Christian centres have a theme of forgiving people. Coventry Cathedral was bombed to ruins during the Second World War and then built again. It has a theme of peace. Taizé in France is an ecumenical centre, where different Christians can meet together for prayer and worship.

In the Roman Catholic Church, if a person wants to be forgiven for something they have done wrong, they can go to confession (the Sacrament of Reconciliation). They tell a priest what they have done wrong. The priest shows the person how to be sorry and be forgiven.

Christians believe that the service of Holy Communion, also called Mass or the Lord's Supper, brings Christians together. It helps them forget arguments. They believe that when they share the bread and wine, they are joining together like different parts of the same body. Most services of Holy Communion include the words:

Though we are many, we are one body, because we all share in one bread.

This shows the Christian belief that people should forget their differences and work together.

Coventry Cathedral puts a special emphasis on peace and forgiveness.

Discussion

Do you think it is right to try to forgive everyone who does wrong, or do you think there are some things that should never be forgiven? Try to give reasons for your answer.

Activity

1 Why do some Christians think other religions are wrong?

2 Christianity is an *evangelical* religion. What does this mean?

3 Write three sentences about Christians and forgiveness.

Glossary words

evangelical

ecumenical movement

Hinduism

Varnashramadharma

All Hindus are born into a social group (**varna**). They stay a member of that group for all their life, until they are reborn. The next life might change things. Someone who has been good, followed the right rules and been kind to others will be reborn into a higher social group. Someone who has done wrong and been selfish will be born into a lower group.

In Hinduism, there are four main varnas. A very old poem called the 'Purusha Sukta', in the **Rig Veda**, tells of how the different varnas were made from different parts of the body of the first man:

> His mouth became the Brahmin; his arms were made into the Warrior, his thighs the People, and from his feet the Servants were born.
>
> (Rig Veda 10.90)

The four varnas

1 **Brahmins** This is the priestly group. They have to keep up the traditions of Hindu worship. They study the Hindu scriptures and teach them to others. They have jobs as priests and teachers.

2 **Kshatriyas** This is the warrior group. Their main duty is to protect and defend other people. They have jobs in government and lead the country.

3 **Vaishyas** This is the group that makes most of the money. They run farms and businesses.

4 **Sudras** This is the servant group. They work to support members of the other varnas. They might be cooks or tailors or bus drivers.

In many Hindu families, sons and daughters are still expected to marry someone from the same varna. There are still rules about which people can share meals with others.

Hindus often say that all of the different groups are equal. They are all just as important as each other. But in real life, not all the groups have the same respect for each other. Most people would like to be Brahmins, who get the best education. Sudras do not have the same chances to become rich or to be educated or to travel. A special Hindu rite called the Sacred Thread ceremony is done for Brahmins, Kshatriyas and Vaishyas, but never for Sudras. Sudras are not allowed to study the Vedas (the holy books). In some parts of India, members of lower groups are not allowed to go into the temples for worship, because it is believed that they are 'unclean' and that their presence will make the temple dirty for everyone else.

The harijans

In the past, some people were thought to be so dirty that they did not have a varna at all. They had jobs like taking away the dead and clearing away rubbish. They were known as 'outcastes' or 'untouchables'. These people were often treated very badly and were not allowed to mix with everyone else.

M K Gandhi thought that this was wrong. He gave them a new name, **harijans**, or 'children of God'. Today they prefer to call themselves **dalits**, which means 'oppressed'. Because of Gandhi's work and the work of many other Hindu leaders, it is now against the law to treat people as 'untouchable'.

Hindus from lower social groups perform services for others, and do the jobs that other Hindus believe are unclean.

Hindus say it is not unfair to have different groups of people. They are the result of past lives. Anyone can get into the top group if they are good and are born next time into a higher varna.

Ashramas

Ashramas are the different stages of life for Hindus. Each stage has its own special duties, or **dharma**. The first stage is the student (**brahmacarya**), when a young person is meant to study the Vedas and be taught by a guru. The next stage is that of the householder (**grihastha**), where people should have sons and work for a living. When the children are grown up, the Hindu is supposed to give up possessions and family ties, in a stage known as **vanaprastha**. Finally, the elderly Hindu becomes a **sannyasin** and lives alone. He meditates on God.

Discussion

Hindus sometimes say that when a society is divided into groups, everyone knows how to behave and can live together in peace. Do you think this is a fair point? Give reasons for your answer.

Activity

1 Write a sentence about each of the four varnas.

2 (a) What was an *untouchable*?

   (b) How did Gandhi change things for people who were *untouchable*?

Glossary words

varna

Rig Veda

harijans

dalits

ashramas

dharma

brahmacarya

grihastha

vanaprastha

sannyasin

Hindu attitudes towards racism

Many races live in India. Hindus have always had to live peacefully with other races. Hindus believe that all people have something in common. The plants, other animals, and humans are all part of the same stream of life. Many Hindus therefore believe that it is wrong to be prejudiced against someone just because of their race.

But Hindus can be just as prejudiced as other people. Many Hindus prefer not to eat with people who are not Hindus. There are still many prejudices within Hinduism between people of different skin colours. When people are looking for a husband or wife, they often say that they want a partner with a light skin colour. These attitudes are hard to change.

The role of women in Hindu society

In Hinduism, men and women have different roles and duties. Each has a different dharma to follow. If families do not have enough money to send all their children to school, they send the boys and not the girls. This is because the boys will have to find jobs, but the girls can work in the home. This might seem unfair. But a Hindu would say that if the woman is good, she could be a man in the next life.

Women should be good wives and mothers. They should do what their husbands ask, and take care of the home and the cooking. They should copy the example of Sita, the wife of Rama. She followed her husband into all kinds of danger and did not complain.

Women are responsible for worship in the home, and this is very special for them. They are the ones who bring up the children to follow Hinduism. All women should marry and, if possible, have sons. In India, when a woman gets married, she often lives with her parents-in-law and helps with their housework until she has children of her own. Then she and her husband move to their own house. Women belong to their fathers when they are young, then they belong to their husbands, and when they are old they belong to their sons.

Modern Hindus sometimes have different ideas about the role of women. More girls now go to school, and India has had a female Prime Minister. But if a woman never marries, Hindus still think she has failed.

Sita is believed to be the ideal example of a Hindu wife.

Hindu attitudes towards other religions

Hinduism teaches that different religions should respect each other. But there has been prejudice between Hindus and

Muslims. Each religion has beliefs that the other finds hard to accept. Hindus worship many different gods, which Muslims think is wrong because of their belief in one God, Allah. Hindus do not like the Muslim way of killing and eating beef, because of their beliefs that the cow is a sacred animal. These differences sometimes make it difficult for Hindus and Muslims to accept each other.

Hinduism includes many different beliefs. Some Hindus follow Krishna as their god, while others follow Ganesha or a different god. Some Hindus do not believe in God at all. So Hindus have no problem if members of other religions want to worship in their own way and have their own beliefs. Hindus say there are many different paths to God.

The **Ramakrishna Mission** was started by a man called Ramakrishna in the nineteenth century. He taught that all religions were paths to God. At that time some Hindus were becoming Christians, but Ramakrishna said there was no need to change religion. He taught that it was best for people to stay with the religion that was part of their culture.

Hindu beliefs about forgiveness

Hindus believe that everything people do brings its own rewards or punishments, in this life or the next life. So if someone is treated badly, they know that the person who did it will one day be punished. There is no point in staying angry with someone, because the other person will get what they deserve. Hindus believe that looking for revenge hurts the person who has these feelings.

Discussion

Do you agree that all religions are equally true (or false), or do you think that one religion is better than all the others? Give reasons for your answer.

Activity

1 Explain Hindu ideas about the role of women. What do you think a Hindu might say to someone who thought that this was unfair?

2 Explain why Hindus do not try to convert other people to their own beliefs.

Glossary words

Ramakrishna Mission

 Islam

Muslim teachings about equality

The Qur'an teaches that all people are created by Allah and so all people are equal:

> And among His Signs is the creation of the heavens and the earth, and the variations in your languages and your colours; verily in that are Signs for those who know.
>
> (Surah 30:22)

> O mankind! We created you from a single (pair) of a male and a female; and made you into nations and tribes, that ye may know each other (not that ye may despise each other). Verily, the most honoured of you in the sight of Allah is (he who is) the most righteous of you. And Allah has full knowledge and is well-acquainted (with all things).
>
> (Surah 49:13)

Muslim attitudes towards racism

Muslims live all over the world and so there is no excuse for racism or prejudice. Muhammad ﷺ was from the country we now call Saudi Arabia. The first muezzin, chosen by Muhammad ﷺ, was an Ethiopian slave called Bilal.

Racism is important for many Muslims, not because they are racist themselves, but because of the way in which they are often treated by other people.

In his last sermon, Muhammad ﷺ said:

> All mankind is descended from Adam and Eve, an Arab is not better than a non-Arab and a non-Arab is not better than an Arab; a white person is not better than a black person, nor is a black person better than a white person except by piety and good actions. Learn that every Muslim is the brother of every other Muslim and that Muslims form one brotherhood.

The role of women in Muslim society

Islam teaches that men and women are equal. In many Muslim countries, women wear clothes that cover up their bodies and show just their hands and sometimes their face. This is so that men respect women for who they are, rather than for their bodies.

> O Prophet! Tell thy wives and daughters, and the believing women, that they should cast their outer garments over their persons (when abroad): that is most convenient, that they should be known (as such) and not molested. And Allah is Oft-Forgiving, most Merciful.
>
> (Surah 33:59)

Many non-Muslims do not understand Muslim teaching about women and feel that being told to cover up in public, and the way in which they are brought up, is wrong. However, some Muslim women say that being covered gives them freedom because they are protected from being stared at by men.

In Islam, the rights and duties of a woman are equal to those of a man, but they are not the same.

> And women shall have rights similar to the rights against them, according to what is equitable; but men have a degree (of advantage) over them. And Allah is Exalted in Power, Wise.
>
> (Surah 2:228)

> Men are the protectors and maintainers of women, because Allah has given the one more (strength) than the other, and because they support them from their means. Therefore the righteous women are devoutly obedient, and guard in (the husband's) absence what Allah would have them guard. As to those women on whose part ye fear disloyalty and ill-conduct, admonish them

Some Muslim women say that being covered is a statement of freedom.

(first), (next), refuse to share their beds, (and last) beat them (lightly); but if they return to obedience seek not against them means (of annoyance): for Allah is Most High, Great (above you all).

(Surah 4:34)

Men must support the family, while women have children and bring them up. Women have the right:

- to study
- to refuse a marriage
- to divorce
- to inherit
- to keep their own name
- to own property
- to take part in politics
- to run a business.

Muhammad ﷺ stressed the respect that should be shown to women:

Paradise lies at the feet of your mother.

(Sunan An-Nasa'i)

A man asked Prophet Muhammad ﷺ, 'O Messenger of Allah! Who deserves the best care from me?' The Prophet said, 'Your mother.' The man asked, 'Who then?' The Prophet said, 'Your mother.' The man asked yet again, 'Who then?' Prophet Muhammad ﷺ said, 'Your mother.' The man asked once more, 'Who then?' The Prophet then said, 'Your father.'

(Sahih Al-Bukhari)

Discussion

Are there any reasons why women should not be treated equally to men?

Activity

Explain the way in which Islam treats women and the rights and duties they have.

Muslim attitudes towards other religions

Islam teaches that it is the only true religion. Muslims believe that they have a duty to lead other people into the faith:

> Strongest among men in enmity to the Believers wilt thou find the Jews and the Pagans; and nearest among them in love to the Believers wilt thou find those who say, 'We are Christians': because amongst these are men devoted to learning and men who have renounced the world, and they are not arrogant.
>
> (Surah 5:82)

> If anyone desires a religion other than Islam (submission to Allah), never will it be accepted of him; and in the Hereafter he will be in the ranks of those who have lost (all spiritual good).
>
> (Surah 3:85)

Islam teaches that all people are born to be Muslims – this is called **fitrah**. People may belong to other religions but this is because of the way they were brought up. When someone 'converts' to Islam, they are actually coming back to the religion into which they were born.

Muslim beliefs about forgiveness and reconciliation

Allah forgives people who admit that they are wrong and pray to be forgiven. Good is always better than evil:

> Nor can Goodness and Evil be equal. Repel (Evil) with what is better: then will be between whom and thee was hatred become as it were thy friend and intimate!
>
> (Surah 41:34)

Islamic law (Shari'ah) is based on the Qur'an and the belief that Allah is a forgiving judge.

Islamic law (**Shari'ah**) is based on the Qur'an. It states how people are to be punished for crimes which they commit against other people.

Shari'ah has very strict rules to protect the person who is being judged, to make sure that they have a fair trial and that the punishment is correct:

- People must be tried by a legal court.
- Murder of a robbery victim is punished by death.
- Bodily harm of a robbery victim is punished by cutting off a hand and a foot.
- Less serious crimes are punished by prison sentences.

Allah is merciful and forgives people, so Muslims believe they must follow this example:

> Hold to forgiveness; command what is right; but turn away from the ignorant.
>
> (Surah 7:199)

> Those who are kind and considerate to Allah's creatures, Allah bestows His kindness and affection on them.
>
> (Abu Dawud, Tirmidhi)

Discussion

Are there any crimes which even religious people might not want to forgive?

Activity

Write a sentence about: (a) *Shari'ah* (b) what Muslims believe about other religions.

Glossary words

fitrah

Shari'ah

Jewish teachings about equality and racism

Jewish teachings remind Jews that they were once held in Egypt as slaves. Because the Jewish people were treated as unequals in a foreign land, Jews should always welcome people from other countries and races and treat them as equals.

> When a proselyte (a convert to Judaism) dwells among you in your land, do not taunt him. The proselyte who dwells with you shall be like a native among you, and you shall love him like yourself, for you were aliens in the land of Egypt – I am HASHEM, your G-d.
>
> (Leviticus 19:33–34)

Jews believe that they should live peacefully with other people. This passage from Isaiah shows the hope for peace. It describes how G-d will end all arguments and disagreements, and people will no longer need weapons:

> It will happen in the end of days: The mountain of the Temple of HASHEM will be firmly established as the head of the mountains, and it will be exalted above the hills, and all nations will stream to it. Many peoples will go and say, 'Come let us go to the Mountain of HASHEM, to the Temple of the G-d of Jacob, and He will teach us of His ways and we will walk in His paths'. For from Zion will the Torah come forth, and the word of HASHEM from Jerusalem. He will judge among the nations, and will settle the arguments of many peoples. They shall beat their swords into plowshares and their spears into pruning hooks; nation will not lift sword against nation and they will no longer study warfare.
>
> (Isaiah 2:2–4)

Judaism says that when G-d created Adam, he took soil from the four corners of the earth and used dark, light, red and yellow soil to make the first human. Everyone is descended from Adam, so no-one can say 'my father is better than your father'.

Different languages in the world are explained by the story of the Tower of Babel (Genesis 11:6–9). Judaism also suggests that the different races in the world came from the three sons of Noah.

Jewish persecution

Jews have been the victims of persecution for 2,000 years. Jews were driven out of Israel in the sixth century BCE and after the destruction of the Temple in 70 CE. They were driven out of Spain in 1492 CE, and during the **Shoah** (Holocaust) of the Second World War (1939–45) six million Jews were killed. For all these centuries, Jews were persecuted because of their race and their religion. This is called **anti-semitism**: 'hatred of the Jews'. Because of this terrible history of prejudice, Judaism is totally against racism. Jews are encouraged to fight against any kind of prejudice and discrimination. It is the responsibility of society to make sure that everyone, of every colour, race, religion, ability or disability, rich or poor, is treated equally.

The role of women in Jewish society

In Orthodox Judaism, women sit separately from men in synagogue services and do not take an active part. Only men are bound by the 613 mitzvot (laws). In Progressive synagogues, women often take part in services.

At the Shabbat service on Friday night, the husband tells his wife how valuable she is:

> An accomplished woman who can find? Far beyond pearls is her value. Her husband's heart relies on her, and he shall lack no fortune. She bestows goodness upon him, never evil, all the days of her life…. Her children have risen and praised her; her husband, and he extolled her:

In the Shabbat service a husband tells his wife how valuable she is to him.

'Many women have amassed achievement, but you surpassed them all.' Grace is false, and beauty vain; a woman who fears HASHEM, she should be praised. Give her the fruits of her hands; and let her be praised in the gates by her very own deeds.

(Proverbs 31:10–31)

Some Jewish women feel that statements such as these show that they are not equal to men. They suggest that women belong only in the home. Some people say that the traditional view of women dates back to the punishment of Eve in the Garden of Eden when she picked the fruit of the Tree of Knowledge and gave it to Adam:

To the woman He said, 'I will greatly increase your suffering and your childbearing; in pain shall you bear children. Yet your craving shall be for your husband, and he shall rule over you.'

(Genesis 3:16)

Progressive Jews try to treat all men and women in the same way. They pray and worship together, and women can become rabbis.

Discussion

Do you think telling someone how valuable they are is the same as treating them equally? Which would you prefer?

Activity

1 What is *prejudice?*

2 What is *discrimination?*

3 Explain how Jews have been persecuted.

Glossary words

Shoah

anti-Semitism

Jewish attitudes towards other religions

Jews say that all people should follow their own religion because this will please G-d. They believe that everyone should follow the **Noachide Code**. The Noachide Code has seven commandments. These seven commandments were given to Noah by G-d after the flood:

● Worship only G-d.
● Do not blaspheme.
● Do not murder.
● Do not steal.
● Do not commit adultery.
● Do not be cruel to animals.
● Establish a system of law and order so that everyone can live together in harmony.

Jews believe that all humans come from Adam and Eve. This means that all people are equal, whatever their beliefs:

> The man called his wife's name Eve, because she had become the mother of all the living.
>
> (Genesis 3:20)

Judaism teaches Jews to remember the time when they lived in a strange country, Egypt. G-d did not wish the early Jews to treat people of other religions badly:

> You shall not reject an Edomite, for he is your brother; you shall not reject an Egyptian, because you were a sojourner in his land. Children who are born to them in the third generation may enter the congregation of HASHEM.
>
> (Deuteronomy 23:8–9)

Jews believe that they should work to help other people, especially as they try to serve G-d:

> I am HASHEM; I have called you with righteousness; I will strengthen your hand; I will protect you; I will set you for a covenant to the people, for a light to the nations; to open blind eyes; to remove a prisoner from confinement, dwellers in darkness from a dungeon.
>
> (Isaiah 42:6–7)

Jews do not try to get people to convert to Judaism. In fact, they try to persuade

People who are born Jews are required by Judaism to follow its mitzvot and customs.

people *not* to convert to Judaism. People should follow their own religion, guided by the Noachide Code. Only people who are born Jews (the children of a Jewish mother) have to follow the mitzvot and customs of Judaism. If someone insists on being converted they have to study Hebrew and Jewish laws and customs. Women have to go to the mikveh and, if the convert is a man, he has to be circumcised. Finally, the convert has to go to a Beth Din (Jewish Court) to be tested by three rabbis.

Jewish beliefs about forgiveness and reconciliation

The rabbis said that everyone should ask to be forgiven for their sins on the day before they died. People asked how they could know when they were about to die, and they answered, 'Exactly, so you must do this every day'. Jews are told:

> You shall not hate your brother in your heart; you shall reprove your fellow and do not bear a sin because of him. You shall not take revenge and you shall not bear a grudge against members of your people; you shall love your fellow as yourself – I am HASHEM.
>
> (Leviticus 19:17–18)

Criminals should be brought to a proper court.

Jews believe that they should forgive other people but that they cannot forgive on behalf of others. When he was asked if he could forgive the Nazis for the Holocaust, Rabbi Hugo Gryn said that only G-d could forgive their crimes.

Discussion

Are there circumstances in which even religious people might feel that they were not able to forgive a criminal?

Activity

1 What is the *Noachide Code?*

2 Write a paragraph about how someone might convert to Judaism.

Glossary words

Noachide Code

Practice GCSE questions

Christianity

(a) Describe and explain Christian beliefs about the truth of other world religions. (8 marks)

(b) Explain how Christian beliefs might affect someone's attitude towards people of other races. (7 marks)

(c) 'People are not the same; there is no point in trying to make everyone equal.'
Do you agree? Give reasons to support your answer, and show that you have thought about different points of view. You must refer to Christianity in your answer. (5 marks)

Hinduism

(a) Describe and explain Hindu beliefs about the truth of other world religions. (8 marks)

(b) Explain how Hindu beliefs might affect someone's attitude towards people of other races. (7 marks)

(c) 'People are not the same; there is no point in trying to make everyone equal.'
Do you agree? Give reasons to support your answer, and show that you have thought about different points of view. You must refer to Hinduism in your answer. (5 marks)

Islam

(a) Describe and explain Muslim beliefs about the truth of other world religions. (8 marks)

(b) Explain how Muslim beliefs might affect someone's attitude towards people of other races. (7 marks)

(c) 'People are not the same; there is no point in trying to make everyone equal.'
Do you agree? Give reasons to support your answer, and show that you have thought about different points of view. You must refer to Islam in your answer. (5 marks)

Judaism

(a) Describe and explain Jewish beliefs about the truth of other world religions. (8 marks)

(b) Explain how Jewish beliefs might affect someone's attitude towards people of other races. (7 marks)

Tips

For all four questions

In part **(a)**, you need to describe and explain how members of the religion you are studying feel about other world religions. Perhaps they think that their religion is the only true one, and that they have a duty to work as missionaries and to try to gain converts. Perhaps they think that other religions also hold some truth, and that people should be free to worship in the way that they want. You need to explain their views, and give reasons where you can.

In part **(b)**, you should think about how religious beliefs might affect someone's attitude to issues of race. You might write about attitudes towards racial prejudice, and the reasons why religious believers hold these attitudes. You might be able to support your points with quotations from sacred texts, or with the example of well-known people who have dealt with the issue of racism.

In part **(c)**, you are being tested on your evaluative skill. You should think about whether equality means that everyone has to be the same, or whether it means something different. You need to explain how a religious believer would answer this question, and also give your own point of view, backed up with reasons explaining why these are your opinions.

(c) 'People are not the same; there is no point in trying to make everyone equal.'
Do you agree? Give reasons to support your answer, and show that you have thought about different points of view. You must refer to Judaism in your answer. (5 marks)

UNIT 9

Religion, Poverty and Wealth

Introduction

The causes of hunger, poverty and disease

In the past, people only knew about the poor people they could see around them. But today, because of television, newspapers, radio and the internet, we know what life is like for poor people all around the world. We know if there is a famine in Africa or an earthquake in India. We know that other people have much less money than we do. We also know that the way we live affects people on the other side of the world. The things we buy, the ways we vote and the ways we use our money can make a big difference to other people.

The North–South divide

In the world today, most rich people live North of the Equator, and most poor people live in the South. The big differences between ways of life for the rich and the poor have become known as the **North–South divide**. Poor countries are often known as the 'developing world'.

People in rich or **developed countries** often have problems because they eat too much. They have to try to lose weight by eating less. Houses are safe and warm, and everyone has clean water. People have different clothes for doing different things. They throw away their clothes when the fashions change. They can go to school until they are adults, and can often choose between jobs to go to. If they are ill, it is easy to find health care.

In **developing countries**, it is hard to find food. People starve, or become ill because they do not have the right sort of food. Around 1.1 billion people do not have safe, clean water. Many live in shacks made from other people's rubbish. Some have no homes at all. Many never go to school, and never learn to read. This is a big problem for women. There is very

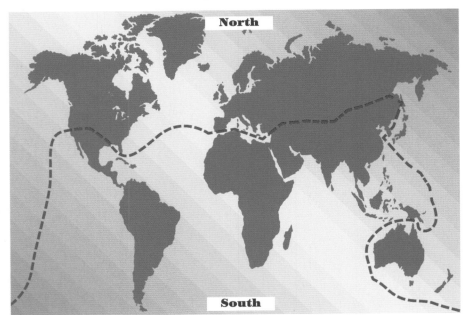

Countries in the North are, in general, much richer and more powerful than those in the South.

little health care. In the poorest countries, a quarter or more of all children die before reaching the age of five.

People who are poor quickly become even poorer. Poor families have more children, to help them with the work and to make sure that enough children live to look after the parents when they become old. Poor countries need more medicine, because disease spreads more quickly. Poor countries do not have emergency supplies to help people if there is a flood or a crop fails.

Poor countries often end up owing rich countries money. They have to borrow to keep people alive. Then they do not have enough to pay it back.

The rich countries have all the power. They have the factories, they own the mines, and they run the banks. They decide how world trade is going to work. They make rules that are unfair for the poor. Aid agencies (charities) often say that the rich countries will have to change their attitudes and their laws before anything gets better for the poor.

Glossary words

North–South divide

developed countries

developing countries

Christianity

Christian teaching about concern for the poor

Christianity teaches that all those who love God must care for the poor. It is not a choice.

The Bible teaches that God will judge people by looking at the way they care for the poor. The parable of the Sheep and the Goats in Matthew's Gospel (Chapter 25) teaches that God knows how much people do for the poor. Only those who care for others will go to heaven.

In the Old Testament, the prophets tell people that they must care for the poor or God will punish them. The Old Testament laws tell people how to make sure that they are fair to poor people:

> If one of your countrymen becomes poor and is unable to support himself among you, help him as you would an alien or a temporary resident, so that he can continue to live among you. You must not lend him money at interest or sell him food at a profit.
>
> (Leviticus 25:35,37)

The teaching of Jesus

When Jesus began his teaching, he told everyone why he had come, and what he was planning to do:

> The Spirit of the Lord is on me,
> because he has anointed me
> to preach good news to the poor.
> He has sent me to proclaim freedom for the prisoners
> and recovery of sight for the blind,
> to release the oppressed,
> to proclaim the year of the Lord's favour.
>
> (Luke 4:18–19)

All of the gospel writers show that Jesus taught about caring for the poor. For Jesus, the poor were just as important as the rich:

Christianity teaches that people cannot be true believers if they do nothing to help the poor.

Looking at his disciples, he said:
'Blessed are you who are poor,
for yours is the kingdom of God.
Blessed are you who hunger now,
for you will be satisfied.
Blessed are you who weep now,
for you will laugh.'

(Luke 6:20–21)

Christian concern about the poor includes everyone, whether they live in the same street or in a different part of the world. The Bible teaches that people who ignore the poor cannot have a real love for God:

If anyone has material possessions and sees his brother in need but has no pity on him, how can the love of God be in him?

(1 John 3:17)

Giving to charity in Christianity

Christians give to charity in different ways. Some give money every month to the charities they support. This is a good way of giving, because it means that the charities know how much money to expect, and they can plan projects knowing that they will be able to fund them.

In the Bible, Paul wrote to the Christians in Corinth telling them that they should keep some of their money to give to the poor, and not spend it all:

On the first day of every week, each one of you should set aside a sum of money in keeping with his income, saving it up...

(1 Corinthians 16:2)

Some Christians keep a small charity box in their homes and they put money into it regularly. They might also give money to the local church, and some of this money is used for helping the poor. Christians often work for charity in other ways too. They might work in a local charity shop, or bake cakes for a charity stall in the local market, or knit for babies in developing countries. Jesus taught that the size of the gift is not important:

As he looked up, Jesus saw the rich putting their gifts into the temple treasury. He also saw a poor widow put in two very small copper coins. 'I tell you the truth,' he said, 'this poor widow has put in more than all the others. All these people gave their gifts out of their wealth; but she out of her poverty put in all she had to live on.'

(Luke 21:1–4)

Some charities support sick animals and some care for children or give money to medical research. When they are choosing a charity to support, Christians are likely to look for something that has a Christian background. They might choose a charity such as Christian Aid, CAFOD or Tearfund.

Discussion

Christianity teaches that people should sell all they have and give the money to the poor. Do you think this is right?

Activity

1 Look up the following passages in the Bible. For each one, write in your own words what you think it is saying:

(a) Matthew 25:31–46

(b) Mark 10:21

(c) James 2:14–17.

2 Find out more about the work of a Christian aid agency, such as CAFOD, Christian Aid or Tearfund.

Christian teaching about the right uses of money

People need money so that they can have somewhere to live and enough to eat. But Christianity teaches that money can often become too important to people, and make them greedy. They want too much, and forget about people in need. Thinking about money can make them forget about God. In the Sermon on the Mount, Jesus taught:

> No-one can serve two masters. Either he will hate the one and love the other, or he will be devoted to the one and despise the other. You cannot serve both God and Money.
>
> (Matthew 6:24)

The Bible also says:

> For the love of money is a root of all kinds of evil.
>
> (1 Timothy 6:10)

In New Testament times, people often thought that if someone had a lot of money, it showed that God was pleased with him or her. But people who were poor were treated with less respect.

Jesus said it was wrong to be too fond of money. Money can give people a very happy and comfortable life, but it does not last for ever. When a rich person dies, he or she cannot take their money with them to heaven.

> Then he said to them, 'Watch out! Be on your guard against all kinds of greed; a man's life does not consist in the abundance of his possessions.'
>
> And he told them this parable: 'The ground of a certain rich man produced a good crop. He thought to himself, "What shall I do? I have no place to store my crops."
>
> 'Then he said, "This is what I'll do. I will tear down my barns and build bigger ones, and there I will store all my grain and my goods. And I'll say to myself, 'You have plenty of good things laid up for many years. Take life easy; eat, drink and be merry.'"

> 'But God said to him, "You fool! This very night your life will be demanded from you. Then who will get what you have prepared for yourself?"
>
> 'This is how it will be with anyone who stores up things for himself but is not rich towards God.'
>
> (Luke 12:15–21)

In Mark's Gospel, a story is told of when a rich young man asked Jesus what he should do in order to get to heaven. He told Jesus that he had tried all his life to be good.

> Jesus looked at him and loved him. 'One thing you lack,' he said. 'Go, sell everything you have and give to the poor, and you will have treasure in heaven. Then come, follow me.' At this the man's face fell. He went away sad, because he had great wealth.
>
> (Mark 10:21–22)

Some people think that when Jesus said this, he was exaggerating in order to make a point. They think he meant that people should try not to be too greedy. But other people think that Jesus really did mean that they should sell all they have and give the money to the poor. Some Christians, such as St Francis of Assisi, have followed this teaching. They have given all their money to the poor so that they can give their lives to God instead.

Monks and nuns usually give up everything except for a few clothes and religious objects, as a way of putting Jesus' teaching into practice.

Christian teaching about moral and immoral occupations

Christianity does not say that some jobs are allowed and others are not allowed. But many Christians try to choose a career that fits in with their beliefs. They might try to find a job helping other people. For example, they might become doctors or nurses or teachers, or they might join the police, or work to get fair treatment for others. Christians do not choose jobs that might hurt others, such as jobs in gambling or pornography.

The internet is a useful way of finding out about different companies. They might use animal testing, or they might not pay people a fair wage, or they might be very good about the way they treat the environment. A Christian could find out more about a company before he or she applied to work there.

Discussion

Do you think people today treat the poor with less respect than the rich? Why might this happen?

Activity

1 What does Christianity teach about money and greed?

2 Do you think Christians should sell all they have and give the money to the poor? Give reasons for your answer.

St Francis of Assisi came from a rich family, but because of his Christian faith he gave all his wealth to the poor. His father was furious with him.

Christians believe that the main use of money should be for helping other people. Christians should only keep what they really need. Any extra money should be given to someone who has less.

Sometimes people say that Christian churches should not own land, expensive buildings and gold and silver. They say Christians should sell all this and give away the money. But other people say that it is important to show respect to God with beautiful things. They say the churches need money so that people have a place of worship and properly trained ministers.

Hinduism

Hindu teaching about moral and immoral occupations

In Hinduism, there is a social system where people are divided into different groups, known as **varnas** (see page 146). Each of these groups has its own rules, known as **dharma**. A family will stay in the same varna, because the children are born into that social group.

The Brahmins are the priests and the teachers. The Kshatriyas are the warriors, rulers, and leaders of society. The Vaishyas work in trade and business. Sudras work with their hands in jobs such as building. A 'good' job for a Hindu is the job that is right for the class into which he or she is born. Many trades and businesses are handed down through a family. Most people in India do the same kind of work that their fathers and grandfathers did before them.

In a village, everyone knows that they need each other. The farmers need the drivers, and the teachers need the rubbish collectors. But at the same time people think some jobs are 'higher' than others. To Hindus this is fair, because someone who does his or her job well can be born into a higher group in the next life.

The Bhagavad Gita, a Hindu book, explains the kinds of work that fit the different groups:

> The works of Brahmins, Kshatriyas, Vaishyas and Shudras are different, in harmony with the three powers of their born nature.

> The works of a Brahmin are peace; self-harmony, austerity and purity; loving-forgiveness and righteousness; vision and wisdom and faith.

> These are the works of a Kshatriya: a heroic mind, inner fire, constancy, resourcefulness, courage in battle, generosity and noble leadership.

> Trade, agriculture and the rearing of cattle is the work of a Vaishya. And the work of the Shudra is service.

A 'right' job is one that is right for someone's social group. So it would be right for a Brahmin to be a priest and wrong for him to be a shoemaker. It would be right for a Sudra to drive a bus but wrong for him to become a teacher. A 'wrong' job is one that takes the Hindu outside his or her own group. Not everyone agrees with this – a lot of Hindus say it is old-fashioned and people should be able to choose any kind of job.

But some kinds of job go against Hindu ideas of right and wrong. Hindus believe that women should dress modestly, and so a Hindu woman would not be a fashion model. Most Hindus are vegetarian, and so they would not be butchers.

Hindu teaching about the right use of money

One of the main aims of Hindu life is called **artha**. The aim is to earn money to look after members of the family who need it. Hindus are allowed to pray for money. At the festival of Divali, Hindu businessmen pray to the goddess Lakshmi, asking her to help to make them rich.

But this does not mean that Hindus can be greedy, or think about money more than they think about other important things. When a Hindu is a student, he is meant to live a very simple life, so that he learns how to live on very little. He should learn that the most important things in life cannot be bought. It is more important to be wise, to love God and to care for other people.

When the student has a home and family of his own, he will remember this. He should earn money for his family.

Lakshmi, the goddess of wealth, is worshipped at Divali in the hope that she will bring money.

Discussion

Are there some kinds of jobs that you would never do, because you think they are morally wrong? Explain your reasons.

Activity

1 Write a sentence about each of the different Hindu social groups (varnas). Do you think this system would make people happy, or unhappy? Give reasons for your answer.

2 Explain Hindu views about the right attitude towards money.

Glossary words

varnas

dharma

artha

Hindus think it is important to look after old people and relations who are poor. Many Hindus who live in other countries still send some of their money back to India to help their families.

Hindu books teach that money does not make people happy. Money is good and useful, but it should not be allowed to take over.

Giving to charity

Giving to the poor is a way of life for Hindus in India. Many people are very poor.

Anyone who has a little more than he or she needs should share it with those who have less. People with some money give jobs to poorer people. They are employed to sweep the yard, to do the washing and so on. Hindus think it is better to give someone a job than just to give them charity.

Hindus can build up good **karma** for themselves, so that they will be rewarded in future lives. If Hindus give money to beggars, the giver will be rewarded for this good deed in later life or in a future rebirth. The beggar might have been their own brother or sister in a past life.

Many Hindus believe that if people are poor, it is their own fault because they must have done wrong in a past life.

But Hindus still try to help them. **Dana**, or giving, is a part of everyday life. Many Hindus give a little money to the poor before their own main meal each day. This reminds them of the need to share with others. Hindus do not often throw away clothes or shoes that they are tired of wearing, because there is always someone who would be glad to have them.

Mahatma Gandhi taught that it is wrong to think that a poor person is only getting what he or she deserves. He believed that every person was a part of God. Gandhi taught that helping others was the best way to find God.

In India, there are many different charities for those in need. Some were started by Hindus. Rich Hindus often give large amounts of money to schools or hospitals, and Hindus in other countries often send money back to India to try and help people there who are poor.

Hindus in India see people who live in poverty every day. They believe that in a former life, a beggar might have been their own brother or sister.

- The **Hindu Mission Hospital** in Chennai, India, for example, gives health care for people and is free for the poor. The staff give injections to stop children catching diseases. There is a clinic for fitting artificial limbs, an eye clinic, and a clinic for leprosy. The hospital staff also take medicines and health education out to people in the villages who cannot get to hospital.
- **Prison Fellowship India** is a charity that works to help prisoners and their families. It runs children's homes, to take care of children whose parents are in prison. It teaches prisoners a trade so that they can get a job when they leave prison.
- Disasters, floods and famines happen quite often in India. On 26 January 2001, a severe earthquake hit Gujarat in India, and left hundreds of people dead and many more homeless. Organisations such as **CAF India** give emergency medicines, food and shelter for the victims. This is the sort of work that Hindus might choose to support.

Discussion

If you saw beggars and people who did not have enough to eat outside your house every day, do you think your attitude to the poor would change? Would you become more caring, or do you think you would stop noticing them?

Activity

1 Explain why Hindus believe that it is important to give to the poor.

2 Do you think it is right, or wrong, for rich Hindus to have servants? Give reasons for your answer.

Glossary words

karma

dana

Islam

Muslim teaching about poverty and zakah

All wealth comes from Allah and it is for everyone's benefit. One of the Five Pillars of Islam, **zakah**, is to do with wealth. Zakah is giving a set amount of money to help others. By doing this, the giver makes the rest of his money pure.

> And be steadfast in prayer and regular in charity: and whatever good ye send forth for your souls before you, ye shall find it with Allah: for Allah sees well all that ye do.
>
> (Surah 2:110)

Zakah is 2.5% of the income and savings of all Muslims after they have taken care of their family. It is not charity which people can choose to to give. Rich people pay more than poor people – only very poor people pay nothing. Zakah means that the rest of the money you have cannot harm you.

In a Muslim country zakah is a type of social security: it means that food, clothing, housing, medicine and education can be provided for every person:

> Alms are for the poor and the needy, and those employed to administer the (funds); for those whose hearts have been (recently) reconciled (to the Truth); for those in bondage and in debt; in the cause of Allah; and for the wayfarer.
>
> (Surah 9:60)

Extra zakah is given at the festivals of Id-ul-Fitr and Id-ul-Adha. Charity, or **sadaqah,** can also be given when someone is in need:

> It is not righteousness that ye turn your faces towards East or West; but it is righteousness – to believe in Allah and the Last Day, and the Angels and the Book, and the Messengers; to spend of your substance, out of love for Him, for your kin, for orphans, for the needy, for the wayfarer, for those who ask, and for the ransom of slaves; to be steadfast in prayer, and practise regular charity, to fulfil their contracts which ye have made; and to be firm and patient, in pain (or suffering) and adversity, and throughout all periods of panic. Such are the people of truth, the God-fearing.
>
> (Surah 2:177)

Charity should always be given privately – it should not be a way of showing off:

> There is a man who gives charity and he conceals it so much that his left hand does not know what his right hand spends.
>
> (Hadith)

Mullahs offer bread and water to pilgrims during Id al-Fitr.

People should not boast about how much charity they give. The only time when this allowed is if it is to set an example for other people to follow:

> Every day, each person has two angels near him who have descended from heaven. One says, 'O Allah!, compensate the person who gives to charity', the other says, 'O Allah! Inflict a loss on the person who withholds his money.'

Discussion

Do you think it is better to choose when to give money to others and how much? Or are there advantages in having a religious obligation to give a certain amount of money?

Activity

Write a paragraph explaining what *zakah* is and how it works.

Glossary words

zakah

sadaqah

Muslim teaching about moral and immoral occupations

Muslims must live according to the Qur'an. Some things are forbidden.

Lending money is not allowed if the lender benefits from interest (**riba**):

> That which ye lay out for increase through the property of (other) people, will have no increase with Allah.
>
> (Surah 30:39)

When people do owe money, Muslims should try to help the debtor:

> If the debtor is in a difficulty, grant him time till it is easy for him to repay. But if ye remit it by way of charity, that is best for you if ye only knew.
>
> (Surah 2:280)

There are Muslim banks where Muslims can borrow money without the bank making interest on the loan.

A Muslim bank

Gambling and lotteries are not allowed in Islam:

> O ye who believe! Intoxicants and gambling ... are ... Satan's handiwork; eschew such (abomination) that ye may prosper.
>
> (Surah 5:91)

This has led to problems in some countries where lottery money is given to charity. Many Muslims feel that they cannot take this money to use for building a new mosque or school.

Muslims in the United Kingdom work to raise money for their mosque, where it is given to the poor. They also send money to Muslim communities abroad. Muslim charities such as Muslim Aid and Islamic Relief work to help people in developing countries.

> The generous man is near God, near Paradise, near men and far from Hell, and the ignorant man who is generous is dearer to God than a worshipper who is miserly.
>
> (Hadith)

Work is an essential part of Islamic life.

> But Allah has created you and your handiwork!
>
> (Surah 37:96)

The Qur'an also includes the work that Muslims should not do. Muslims cannot profit from alcohol or gambling, from brothels or prostitution:

> Women impure are for men impure, and men impure for women impure, and women of purity are for men of purity, and men of purity are for women of purity
>
> (Surah 24:26)

nor from lying, fraud or burglary:

> And do not eat up your property among yourselves for vanities, nor use it as bait for the judges, with intent that ye may eat up wrongfully and knowingly a little of (other) people's property.
>
> (Surah 2:188)

Salah (prayer) is an important part of a Muslim's daily life.

Praying five times a day means that Muslims stop their normal activities to think about Allah. This is particularly so at Salat-ul-Jumu'ah, the weekly prayers at noon on Fridays. Islam does not have a day of rest but all Muslims should attend these prayers each Friday and hear the khutbah (talk) given by the Imam.

The fast of Ramadan also brings people closer together and helps them to focus on God.

Discussion

Consider Muslim arguments about not accepting money that has come from gambling or a lottery. Do you think that religious principles should come before the possible benefits to people and to the community?

Activity

Explain why Muslims might not accept charity money from a lottery.

Glossary words

riba

The two Pillars of Salah (prayer) and Sawm (fasting from sunrise to sunset through the month of Ramadan) are also important parts of Muslim teaching about work.

Judaism

Jewish teaching about poverty and tzedaka

Jews are expected to give a tenth of their wealth as **tzedaka** (righteousness). This money is owed to the poor, so not to give it to them is robbery. Even the very poorest people give something as tzedaka.

The worst way to give tzedaka is to hand someone the money; the best way is to lend it to them indefinitely and without interest. The money should help a poor person to become self-supporting so that they no longer need help:

> The best way of giving is to help a person help themselves so that they may become self-supporting.
>
> (Maimonides)

> If there shall be a destitute person among you, any of your brethren in any of your cities, in your land that HASHEM, your G-d, gives you, you shall not harden your heart or close your hand against your destitute brother. Rather, you shall open your hand to him; you shall lend him his requirement, whatever is lacking to him.
>
> (Deuteronomy 15:7)

Many Jews have collection boxes called **pushkes**. Jews also try to make sure that any excess money is used for the poor:

> When you reap the harvest of your land, you shall not complete your reaping to the corner of your field, and the gleanings of your harvest you shall not take. You shall not pick the undeveloped twigs of your vineyard; and the fallen fruit of your vineyard you shall not gather; for the poor and the proselyte shall you leave them – I am HASHEM, your G-d.
>
> (Leviticus 19:9–10)

People must never waste or give away so much money that they become poor. This is wrong because then other people have to look after them:

> It is better to make your Sabbath like a weekday than to need other people's support.

Jews should not be concerned about creating large amounts of money:

> Do not weary yourself to become rich; forbear from your own understanding.
>
> (Proverbs 23:4)

> As goods increase, so do those who consume them; what advantage, then, has the owner except what his eyes see?
>
> (Ecclesiastes 5:10)

Love of money can lead people away from G-d. This passage warns that people should not love their wealth and forget G-d and all he has done for the Jewish people:

> Take care lest you forget HASHEM, your G-d, by not observing His commandments, His ordinances, and His decrees, which I command you today lest you eat and be satisfied, and you build good houses and settle, and your cattle and sheep and goats increase, and you increase silver and gold for yourselves, and everything that you have will increase – and your heart will

Children are encouraged to give part of their pocket money to charity.

THEY'RE NOT ASKING FOR A TON OF MONEY TO SURVIVE THE WINTER.

JUST A TON OF COAL.

Over 100,000 elderly Ukrainian Jews face a desperately difficult winter, where the temperature will go as low as 30 degrees below freezing point. If they spend their tiny pensions (£11 a month) on fuel, they have no money for food.

In the words of 82 year-old Ludmilla Kornikov: "We never had a fancy life, but now it is real poverty. The inflation meant our savings became worthless and now we only have money either for a loaf of bread and a glass of milk or to buy a little coal. Our conditions are very difficult. We have no money to live."

World Jewish Relief is launching an Emergency Winter Relief Appeal which will pay for fuel and other life-saving supplies. Just £40 will buy a ton of coal, which will provide elderly Jews like the Kornikovs with the fuel they're missing for the winter.

Don't leave Ukrainian Jews out in the cold. Please give as generously as you can using the coupon.

WORLD JEWISH RELIEF

WJR EMERGENCY WINTER RELIEF APPEAL
☐ I am sending you a donation of £ _____
Name _____
Address _____
Postcode _____ Tel _____
Please make your cheque payable to World Jewish Relief (Regd. Charity 290 767). Send this coupon to: World Jewish Relief, Drayton House, 30 Gordon Street, London WC1H 0AN.

become haughty and you will forget HASHEM, your G-d, Who took you out of the land of Egypt from the house of slavery.

(Deuteronomy 8:11–14)

Gemilut Hasadim is another form of Jewish charity. It means 'kind actions'. This work might be organisations for Jews such as Jewish Care or the Norwood Orphanages, soup kitchens to feed the hungry and worldwide organisations such as Tzedek, which tries to improve conditions for all people around the world.

Discussion

'All charity should be given anonymously.' Do you agree with this statement? Consider different points of view in your discussion.

Activity

Write a sentence about:

(a) *tzedaka*

(b) *Gemilut Hasadim*.

Glossary words

tzedaka

pushke

Gemilut Hasadim

Jewish teaching about moral and immoral occupations

Work is a very important part of Jewish life and everyone is expected to work:

> By the sweat of your brow shall you eat bread until you return to the ground, from which you were taken; For you are dust, and to dust shall you return.
>
> (Genesis 3:19)

> Great is work. G–d's presence only rested upon the Jewish people when they began occupying themselves with useful work.
>
> (Maimonides)

Work must also leave time for studying the Torah:

> Gather together the people – the men, the women, and the small children, and your stranger who is in your cities – so that they will hear and so that they will learn ... this Torah.
>
> (Deuteronomy 21:12)

Jewish law says that all business transactions must be honest:

> You shall not commit a perversion in justice, in measures of length, weight, or volume. You shall have correct scales, correct weights, correct dry measures, and correct liquid measures – I am HASHEM, your G-d, Who brought you forth from the land of Egypt.
>
> (Leviticus 19:35–36)

Jewish law also makes the person selling responsible for the quality of the goods they sell.

One of the most important parts of Jewish working life is Shabbat, the Sabbath on which no work is done:

> Remember the Sabbath day to sanctify it. Six days shall you work and accomplish all your work; but the seventh day is Sabbath to HASHEM, your G-d; you shall not do any work – you, your son, your daughter, your slave, your maidservant, your animal, and your convert within your gates – for in six days HASHEM made the heavens and the earth, the seas and all that is in them, and He rested on the seventh day. Therefore, HASHEM blessed the Sabbath day and sanctified it.
>
> (Exodus 20:8–11)

There are 39 different types of things which cannot be done on the Sabbath (see below). These include all work, writing, cooking, and travelling except on foot.

Growing and preparing food
Ploughing
Stacking sheaves
Selecting out
Kneading
Sowing
Threshing
Sifting
Cooking
Reaping
Winnowing
Grinding

Making clothing
Sheep shearing
Dyeing
Weaving
Separating threads
Sewing
Washing
Spinning
Removing a finished article
Tying knots
Combining raw materials
Threading a loom
Untying knots
Tearing

Leatherwork and writing
Trapping
Tanning
Cutting
Slaughtering
Scraping
Writing
Flaying skins
Marking out
Erasing

Providing shelter
Building
Demolishing

Creating fire
Kindling a fire
Extinguishing a fire

Work completion
Completing an object or making it usable
Transporting goods
Carrying in a public place

- **Muktzeh** – objects such as work tools and money should not even be handled on the Sabbath.
- **Sh'vut** – you should not ask someone to do something on the Sabbath that you cannot do yourself, unless you ask them in advance.
- **Uvdin d'chol** – weekday things (for example, you should not read business papers).

All these laws can be broken in the case of **pikuakh nefesh**, 'to save life'. This means that almost any law can be broken in order to save life:

> Whoever destroys a single life is considered as if he had destroyed the whole world, and whoever saves a single life as if he had saved the whole world.
>
> (Mishnah)

Non-Jews can work for Jews on the Sabbath if it is for the benefit of health, for example lighting a fire.

Pikuakh nefesh means that the Sabbath laws can be broken in order to save life.

All Jewish businesses must close on the Sabbath. In Jewish hotels, lifts stop automatically at every floor so that people do not have to push buttons.

Discussion

'Having strict religious laws about what can and cannot be done is a disadvantage to religious believers.' What do you think about this statement?

Activity

Write a paragraph explaining what it would be like to be a Jew on the Sabbath.

Glossary words

pikuakh nefesh

Practice GCSE questions

Christianity

(a) Describe Christian teaching about poverty.

(8 marks)

(b) Explain why a Christian might regularly give money to charity. (7 marks)

(c) 'People should look after their own families first rather than giving money to others.' Do you agree? Give reasons to support your answer and show that you have thought about different points of view. You must refer to Christianity in your answer. (5 marks)

Hinduism

(a) Describe Hindu teaching about poverty.

(8 marks)

(b) Explain why a Hindu might regularly give money to charity. (7 marks)

(c) 'People should look after their own families first rather than giving money to others.' Do you agree? Give reasons to support your answer and show that you have thought about different points of view. You must refer to Hinduism in your answer. (5 marks)

Islam

(a) Describe Muslim teaching about poverty.

(8 marks)

(b) Explain why a Muslim might regularly give money to charity. (7 marks)

(c) 'People should look after their own families first rather than giving money to others.' Do you agree? Give reasons to support your answer and show that you have thought about different points of view. You must refer to Islam in your answer. (5 marks)

Judaism

(a) Describe Jewish teaching about poverty.

(8 marks)

(b) Explain why a Jew might regularly give money to charity. (7 marks)

Tips

For all four questions

In part **(a)**, you need to describe the teachings of the religion you are studying, rather than giving your own opinion. What might a religious believer say about why people are poor? Would they blame it on God, or the Devil, or on past lives? For high marks, you should try to explain religious ideas as clearly as you can, and perhaps give some examples.

In part **(b)**, you should show your understanding of giving money to charity. Try to think of several different ideas. You might write about the teachings of the holy books from the religion you are studying.

For part **(c)**, you need to show that you understand people might have different views about this. How might a religious believer answer? What might a non-believer, or someone from a different religion, say in response to this question? Remember, too, to give your own view. It might be the same as one of the ideas you have already expressed, or it might be another, different point of view.

(c) 'People should look after their own families first rather than giving money to others.' Do you agree? Give reasons to support your answer and show that you have thought about different points of view. You must refer to Judaism in your answer. (5 marks)

UNIT 10

Religion, Peace and Justice

Christianity

Christian attitudes towards war

Christians believe that God wants everyone to live in peace. But most Christians also believe that war is sometimes needed, to stop even worse things happening. The Bible gives different views about whether or not war is right. Christians try to decide which is the right view.

In the 13th century, Thomas Aquinas set down some rules, which are known as the **Just War Theory**. They show Christians how to tell if a war is right.

The Just War

Thomas Aquinas said that a war is only 'just', or 'fair', if it keeps to these rules:

1 The war must be started by the people in charge, not by just anyone.
2 People should only go to war for a good reason and not just out of greed or to take revenge.
3 Everything should be done to make sure that at the end of the war, the world is better and more peaceful than it was before.

Later on, other people added extra rules. They said:

4 The war must be a last resort, when every other way of solving the conflict has been tried.
5 People should only use just enough force to win a war. They should not attack people who are not a threat, such as children or old people.

Christians and war today

Christians today still use the Just War rules. Some Christians think that going to war can be the right thing, if the rules for a Just War are kept.

Other people think war is always wrong. They are known as **conscientious objectors** because their consciences tell them to object to war. If their country is at war, they will not fight, but do peaceful things instead, such as nursing. The Quakers are a Christian group who believe that war is never right.

Violence and pacifism

There are different views in the Bible about using violence.

(a) When the Bible says fighting can be right

In the Old Testament, people are often told by God to go to war. Sometimes God tells the people to fight and destroy other tribes. For example, in the book of Joel, the prophet gave this message. He was saying that God wanted the people to get

Some Christians believe that war can be necessary to overcome evil, and to defend the weak.

ready for war, and make weapons out of their farm tools:

> Proclaim this among the nations:
> Prepare for war! ...
> Beat your ploughshares into swords and your pruning hooks into spears.
>
> (Joel 3:9)

One of the Ten Commandments is 'Do not murder', but a lot of people would say that killing in a war is not the same as murder.

(b) When the Bible says fighting is wrong

The Old Testament also says that peace is better than war. The prophets spoke about a time when people could live at peace with each other:

> Nation will not take up sword against nation, nor will they train for war any more.
>
> (Micah 4:3)

The New Testament of the Bible teaches about peace as well. In the Sermon on the Mount, Jesus said that the peacemakers would be called 'children of God'. He taught that people should love each other, and even love their enemies:

> Love your enemies and pray for those who persecute you, that you may be sons of your Father in heaven.
>
> (Matthew 5:44-45)

Pacifism and non-violent protest

Some Christians think that violence is *always* wrong, even if you are being attacked. People who think like this are called **pacifists**. Pacifists do not think that other people should be allowed to get away with any kind of unjust or aggressive behaviour. But they do think that the best way to deal with attacks is to use peaceful methods.

If countries disagree, a pacifist might think it would be best to refuse to trade with the other country, for example, rather than going to war. The countries might have meetings and try to agree on a way to sort out their problem.

Some Christians are pacifists because they believe that the Christian message of love can never allow killing, even in a war.

Non-violent protest is when people try to make their point without fighting. Non-violent protest can be used at other times, as well as during wars. If people want to make a point without using violence, they might try going on marches, making speeches, or using their vote. But in some countries not everyone has the right to do these things.

Discussion

Would you fight in a war to defend your country? Explain why, or why not. You might think it is right to defend the weak and not let the enemy win. Or you might think killing is always wrong, even in a war.

Activity

1 (a) Why did Thomas Aquinas make rules about a Just War?

(b) Do you think these are good rules? Say why, or why not.

2 Write a sentence to explain what a *pacifist* is.

3 What name is given to a person whose conscience tells him or her to object to war?

4 Give two examples of *non-violent protest*.

Glossary words

Just War Theory

conscientious objectors

pacifists

non-violent protest

Christian beliefs about the treatment of criminals

Christianity teaches that people should love each other and forgive their enemies. This might seem to mean that Christians should not punish criminals, but should forgive them instead.

In the Bible, a woman was about to be stoned to death because she had been caught committing adultery. But Jesus said to the people who were waiting to kill her:

> If any one of you is without sin, let him be the first to throw a stone at her.
>
> (John 8:7)

No-one could throw the first stone at the woman, because they all knew they had done wrong things. So the woman was set free.

But Christians think it is important to punish people who break the law. They believe it is right to protect the weak. If people were forgiven every time they committed a crime, then no-one would be safe.

Some Christians believe in capital punishment (the death penalty), because the Bible says it should be used for serious crimes. But other Christians believe that the death penalty is wrong. They say human life is sacred. The criminal should be given the chance to become a better person.

Aims of punishment

Christians believe that punishment has four main aims:

- **Deterrence** – it should act as a warning, so that everyone knows what will happen to them if they break the law. It should put people off committing crimes.
- **Protection** – it should protect people from those who might want to harm them.
- **Retribution** – it should be a way for the victims of the crime to see that the person has been paid back for what he or she has done.
- **Reformation** – it should give the criminal the chance to think about his or her mistakes, and become a better person.

Prison reform

Some Christians have worked to make prisons better places. Elizabeth Fry (see picture opposite) was a Christian who lived from 1780 to 1845. She thought people in prison should have basic human rights. A lot of her work was in a London prison called Newgate. It was well known as a terrible place. She also worked to make things better for criminals who were sent on prison ships to countries such as Australia. They were often kept crowded close together, and many people died. Elizabeth Fry believed that all people are made by God. Because of her work, people in prison were given more space and better food, and they learned skills to help them get jobs when they left prison.

Christian responses to social injustice

'Social injustice' means some members of society are given fewer rights than others. Christians believe that all people matter to God. It is part of Christian belief to try and make the world a fairer place for those who live in it.

The Bible teaches that God notices when people do wrong to the poor and the weak. In the Old Testament, the prophets often spoke out against social injustice, telling the people that God saw what they were doing and would punish them unless they changed their ways.

In the New Testament, Christians are told not to have favourites. They should not treat rich people better than they treat the poor:

> Suppose a man comes into your meeting wearing a gold ring and fine clothes, and a poor man in shabby clothes also comes in.

If you show special attention to the man wearing fine clothes and say, 'Here's a good seat for you', but say to the poor man, 'You stand there' or 'Sit on the floor by my feet', have you not discriminated among yourselves and become judges with evil thoughts?

(James 2:2–4)

The Bible teaches that people from ethnic minorities and immigrants (often called 'aliens' in the Bible) should be treated just the same as family:

When an alien lives with you in your land, do not ill-treat him. The alien living with you must be treated as one of your native-born. Love him as yourself.

(Leviticus 19:33–34)

Elizabeth Fry put her Christian faith into action by campaigning for prisoners to be treated as human beings.

Amnesty International is an organisation that helps people who have been sent to prison unfairly, and many of its members are Christians. Some Christians go to visit people in their local prison, so that the prisoners know somebody cares. Some join groups that try to make prisons better places.

Sometimes, people are treated badly because they have learning difficulties or are disabled. It is harder for them to find jobs and the right houses. Christians try to make things more fair for them, by joining groups such as MENCAP.

In some countries, the police kidnap, torture and execute those who disagree with the government. **Liberation theology** is the name of a Christian movement which tries to help people who live in places like this.

Discussion

Do you think that prisoners today are treated properly? Perhaps you think that prisons are too easy for the people inside. You might think that prison life is too hard. Give reasons for your answer.

Activity

1 Look up Luke 4:18–19. What did Jesus say he had come to do?

2 Find out more about Elizabeth Fry, and write about her work.

Glossary words

Amnesty International

liberation theology

Hinduism

Hindu attitudes towards war

The concept of ahimsa

Ahimsa is one of the most important beliefs for Hindus. It is hard to put into English. It means doing no harm to any other living thing. It also means working hard to make peace, and to stop people treating each other badly.

Most Hindus think that fighting in a war is wrong. They think it will bring bad karma, so the person who fights will be punished in a future life.

But this does not mean that war is never allowed in Hinduism. In the Vedas (Hindu holy books) people often pray to the gods to help them win battles:

> Once shot, fly far away, arrow, sharpened with prayer. Go straight to our foes, and do not leave a single one of them there.
>
> (Rig Veda)

Hindus are divided into different social groups. One of these is called **Kshatriyas**, and they are the warriors. It is the duty, or **dharma**, of Kshatriyas to fight in battles and to defend the people. In the Bhagavad Gita, the god Krishna talks to a soldier called Arjuna in a battle. Arjuna did not want to fight in the battle, even though it was his duty as a member of the warrior class. The enemies were his own family, and Arjuna felt that it would be wrong to kill them in battle. He asked Krishna what he should do:

> Shall I kill with my arrows my grandfather's brother, great Bhisma? Shall my arrows in battle slay Drona, my teacher?
>
> (Bhagavad Gita 2:4)

The god Krishna told Arjuna that he should fight in the battle. It was his duty as a Kshatriya:

> Think thou also of thy duty and do not waver. There is no greater good for a warrior than to fight in a righteous war.
>
> (Bhagavad Gita 2:31)

Some Hindus believe that war is always wrong. They say violence must never be used, because it goes against ahimsa. But others believe that war is sometimes needed. They say fighting in battle is part of the religious duty of Kshatriya Hindus.

The **Laws of Manu** is a very old Hindu book. It tells Hindus about the right ways to behave during wartime. The book says that Kshatriyas should fight, because it is their duty. When they fight, they should only fight other soldiers, and not hurt old people, women or children. They should fight fairly. They must not attack people while they are sleeping or after they have surrendered. Many Hindus believe that these rules are right for all time because right and wrong never change. But others say that the rules do not fit modern wars. Weapons can be sent by computers from far away, so it is impossible to avoid harming people who are not soldiers.

Violence and pacifism

Gandhi was one of the world's most famous Hindus. A **pacifist** is someone who believes that violence is always wrong, and Gandhi was a pacifist.

Gandhi wanted to help people in South Africa and in India, when he saw that they were being treated unfairly. The Indians were being ruled by the British and they wanted to rule India themselves. Gandhi believed that the way to win fair treatment could never be violent. Instead, he set an example of peaceful, non-violent protest. His followers were told to use methods such as sit-ins and demonstrations to make their point. However badly he was treated, Gandhi never used violence. The people who used violence against Gandhi looked bad to the rest of the world.

Gandhi was admired very much for what he did. The British left India in 1947, and the people were free to form their own government.

Gandhi put his belief in ahimsa into practice. He refused to use violence in the struggle to make India independent.

Discussion

Do you think that there are times when it is right to use violence? Explain your answer.

Activity

1 Do you think the old Hindu rules about war can be used in the modern world? If not, how do you think they should be changed? Give reasons for your answer.

2 Explain why people still admire the example set by Mahatma Gandhi.

Glossary words

ahimsa

Kshatriyas

dharma

Laws of Manu

pacifist

Hindu beliefs about the treatment of criminals

Old Hindu books say that in the past, crimes were punished by the local leaders and rulers. The person who had done the crime was sent to the king, and the king decided what should happen as a punishment. It made the country more peaceful and the king was stronger, because everyone liked living with fair rules. Today, it is not possible for this to happen, because there are too many people. There are national laws for everyone.

The Laws of Manu, a very old Hindu book, gives lists of crimes and also the right punishments for them. For example, a shopkeeper who was found guilty of cheating the customers should be fined. Murder is the most serious crime, and Hinduism allows punishment by death.

Hindus believe that people who are never caught for their crimes will still be punished. This is because their bad deeds will bring them bad karma, so they will have bad luck either in this life or in a future life.

Hindus teach that crimes need to be punished for three reasons:

1 **Restraint**: the person is prevented from doing any more crime, which protects the rest of the society.
2 **Retribution** (revenge): society has revenge on the criminal for the wrong that was done.
3 **Reformation**: the punishment should make the criminal a better person.

Hindu responses to social injustice

Hinduism teaches that people belong to different social groups, or **varnas**. Each different group has a different place in society. A person cannot change the group to which he or she belongs, except in a future life. Hindus will try hard to lead a good life so that next time, they are born into a group with more money and more respect.

Hindus think that past lives make things the way that they are. If someone is poor, or disabled, this is because of past behaviour. For many Hindus, then, life does not seem unfair, because everyone deserves the life that they get.

Today, many Hindus no longer care about whether their friends come from one group or another. But in some parts of India it still matters. This can mean that some people are treated in a way that people in the West might regard as very unfair.

Some people have to do jobs that other Hindus think are dirty, such as getting rid of dead animals, taking away rubbish, and clearing drains. Some think that such people will make everyone else dirty, if they are allowed to use the same wells, temples or public transport. So they used to be called 'untouchables', and they had to live apart from everyone else.

Some Hindus, such as Mahatma Gandhi, believed that this sort of treatment is wrong. These Hindus have worked to tell everyone that this is unfair. In 1950 a law was passed to stop people calling anyone 'untouchable', and to stop them being separated from everyone else. Today, they are known as **dalits**, or 'the oppressed' because of the treatment that they have been given. The law in India now says they have to be allowed the same houses, health care and schools as everyone else. But the law does not always change people's feelings about others.

Many Hindus have worked to try and make the world a fairer place for everyone. Hindus have started schools and colleges for women, to try and provide equal education for both sexes. Some Hindus have worked to help the poor and the disabled, by giving money for hospitals and clinics.

Dalits are regarded by some Hindus as impure, because they have to do dirty jobs.

Discussion

Why do you think some people want to keep other people apart from the rest of society? What happens when some people have a lot more than others?

Activity

1 Hindus give three reasons for punishing criminals. Explain what they are, and say which you think is the most important. Try to support your choice with reasons.

2 Explain what a *dalit* is.

Glossary words

varnas

dalits

Islam

Muslim attitudes towards war

The concept of jihad

People often say that **jihad** is a 'Holy War'. This is wrong. Jihad means 'to struggle in the way of Allah'. It is the way every Muslim tries to live in order to carry out Allah's will and to fight against evil. A person who performs jihad is called **Mujahid**.

> The most excellent jihad is the uttering of truth in the presence of an unjust ruler.
>
> (Hadith)

Muslims believe that to fight against evil and to protect Islam, it may be necessary to fight. This fighting is **Harb al-Muqadis** – a Holy War.

> The Prophet was asked about people fighting because they are brave, or in honour of a certain loyalty, or to show off: which of them fights for the cause of Allah? He replied, 'The person who struggles so that Allah's word is supreme is the one serving Allah's cause.'
>
> (Hadith)

Muhammad ﷺ led his followers into battle at the Battle of Badr in 624 CE, to defend the safety of the Muslims in al-Madinah.

Self-defence is a just reason for war, but Muslims must not be the first to attack:

> Fight in the cause of Allah those who fight you, but do not transgress limits; for Allah loveth not transgressors.
>
> (Surah 2:190)

A war cannot be described as jihad if:
- the war is started by a political leader rather than a religious leader
- a person declares war without the support of the Muslim community
- the war is aggressive, not defensive
- peaceful ways of solving the problem have not been tried first
- the purpose of the war is to force people to convert to Islam
- the purpose of the war is to gain land or power
- innocent women and children are put at physical risk
- trees, crops and animals have not been protected
- the war involves the destruction of homes or places of worship.

The Crusades in the 11th to 13th centuries were seen by Christians as a Holy War to recapture Jerusalem from the Muslims. But did Muslims see the Crusades as a jihad?

Jihad is a way to peace. Muslims wish to live in a society where they can worship Allah in peace. According to the Qur'an and the sayings of the Prophet, Muslims must not start a war. If the enemy offers peace, then Muslims must stop fighting.

Violence and pacifism

The word 'Islam' also means 'peace'. This does not mean that Muslims will not fight against injustice or to defend themselves. However, these battles must be fought without hatred, and once the fighting is over peace must be restored.

> Hate your enemy mildly; he may become your friend one day.
>
> (Hadith)

Muslims work towards a world where people can live without being afraid of attack or of evil rulers. There should be no kind of discrimination or prejudice. Muslims believe that by living by Allah's teachings they can help to save humanity from destruction. This struggle is jihad.

Muslims are against any fighting between Muslim countries, as this is completely against jihad.

Discussion

Do you think there are times when pacifism is not the correct response to a situation?

Activity

Write a paragraph explaining what is meant by *jihad*.

Glossary words

jihad

Mujahid

Harb al-Muqadis

Muslim beliefs about the treatment of criminals

Islamic law (**Shari'ah**) is used to judge and punish criminals in many Muslim countries. Shari'ah means the 'way to water', or the source of life.

Islam says that there are three types of sin:
- **shirk** – treating someone or something else as God
- **zalim** – crimes such as murder, theft, suicide and illegal sexual relations
- the third type is lying, swearing and envy.

Only God can forgive, so punishment is a means of protecting society.

Penalties are called hudu, which means 'boundaries'. This is because the boundaries between right and wrong have been crossed.

Punishment of different crimes

Hudu applies to crimes that are listed in the Qur'an or Hadith.
- In a case of **murder**:

> ...if anyone slew a person – unless it be for murder or for spreading mischief in the land – it would be as if he slew the whole people.
>
> (Surah 5:32)

Murder is only allowed if the victim has murdered someone or if they are guilty of speaking against Allah. However, no-one can be killed except by legal means.

- **Adultery** (sex outside of marriage):

> The woman and the man guilty of adultery or fornication – flog each of them with a hundred stripes: let not compassion move you in their case, in a matter prescribed by Allah, if ye believe in Allah and the Last Day: and let a party of the Believers witness their punishment.
>
> (Surah 24:2)

- **Destroying someone's character**:

> And those who launch a charge against chaste women, and produce not four witnesses (to support their allegations) – flog them with eighty stripes; and reject their evidence ever after: for such men are wicked transgressors.
>
> (Surah 24:4)

- **Theft**:

> As to the thief, male or female, cut off his or her hands: a punishment by way of example, from Allah, for their crime.
>
> (Surah 5:38)

Islam allows for the person who has been the victim of the crime to have compensation:

> O ye who believe! The law of equality is prescribed to you in cases of murder: the free for the free, the slave for the slave, the woman for the woman. But if any remission is made by the brother of the slain, then grant any reasonable demand, and compensate him with handsome gratitude. This is a concession and a Mercy from your Lord. After this, whoever exceeds the limits shall be in grave penalty.
>
> (Surah 2:178)

Once a person has been punished, and has asked God to forgive them, they must be treated normally. Allah is forgiving and merciful, and people should be too.

Muslim responses to social injustice

There are three groups of people who require special care and attention: orphans, the needy, and travellers:

> What Allah has bestowed on His Messenger (and taken away) from the people of the townships – belongs to Allah – to his Messenger and to kindred and orphans, the needy and the wayfarer; in order that it may not (merely) make a circuit between the wealthy among you.
>
> (Surah 59:7)

Orphans

Muslims try to arrange for orphans to be brought up by relatives or family.

Orphans should know their family's history and background and receive any property that belonged to their parents:

> To orphans restore their property (when they reach their age), nor substitute (your) worthless things for (their) good ones; and devour not their substance (by mixing it up) with your own. For this is indeed a great sin.
>
> (Surah 4:2)

The needy

The poor, disadvantaged or handicapped are seen as needy people:

> It is not fault in the blind, nor in one born lame, nor in one afflicted with illness.
>
> (Surah 24:61)

Travellers

Travellers are seen as beggars or people who have lost all hope. Islam says they should be helped to return to a normal life.

The elderly

Elderly people are the wealth of Islam because of all the work they have done in their lives. They must be shown great respect:

Thy Lord hath decreed that ye worship none but Him, and that ye be kind to parents. Whether one or both of them attain old age in thy life, say not to them a word of contempt, nor repel them, but address them in terms of honour. And, out of kindness, lower to them the wing of humility, and say: 'My Lord! Bestow on them thy Mercy even as they cherished me in childhood.'

(Surah 17:23–24)

Discussion

Think about the different purposes of punishment, e.g. revenge, retribution, protection. Which of these do you think is the most important? Why?

Activity

Who, according to Islam, are the three groups of people who need special care and attention?

Glossary words

Shari'ah

In some societies elderly people are not valued, but in Muslim society they are shown much respect.

 # Judaism

Jewish attitudes towards war

The concept of Holy War

Several wars are described in the Jewish Scriptures. Some were Holy Wars where the Jews were trying to protect their religion. Others were 'Just Wars' (see page 180).

Judaism says that there are three kinds of wars which must be fought:

1 **Milchemet mitzvah** – this is a war ordered by G-d, and is similar to a Holy War. The conditions for this war are that the enemy has attacked first or that there is a need to prevent an attack.

2 **Milchemet reshut** – an optional war, or a Just War:
   ● The war should be a last resort.
   ● Peaceful attempts to solve the problem should have been tried first.
   ● Civilians should not be harmed.
   ● Damage should be limited.
   No war like this has happened since the fall of the Temple in 70 CE.

3 **Pre-emptive war** – this may only be fought when Israel is just about to be attacked. This happened in 1967, when Israel attacked the airfields of Egypt and Syria in the Six Day War, to try to prevent a long fight.

Jews must protect themselves and other Jews, and help other countries to prevent the spread of war.

Self-defence is allowed:

> If a person intends to kill you, be first to kill him.
>
> (Talmud)

Some of the rules about war are found in the Torah (see Deuteronomy 20:10–13, 19–20).

Judaism teaches that wars must be fought properly and humanely:

> If your foe is hungry, feed him bread; and if he is thirsty, give him water to drink.
>
> (Proverbs 25:21)

'Only G-d can forgive the Nazis for the Holocaust.'

Violence and pacifism

Peace and justice is at the centre of Judaism:

> The world endures on three things – justice, truth and peace.
>
> (Ethics of the Fathers 1:18)

> HASHEM will give might to His nation, HASHEM will bless His nation with peace.
>
> (Psalm 29:11)

> In G-d's eyes the man stands high who makes peace between men – between husband and wife, between parents and children, between management and labour, between neighbour and neighbour. But he stands highest who establishes peace among the nations.
>
> (Talmud)

Shalom – peace – is a Hebrew word which also means 'hello' and 'goodbye'.

Lex Talionis

Lex Talionis is the law of retaliation:

> But if there shall be a fatality, then you shall award a life for a life; an eye for an eye, a tooth for a tooth, a hand for a hand, a foot for a foot.
>
> (Exodus 21:23–24)

It does not mean that if someone cuts off your hand then you should cut off theirs. It is meant to limit the amount of revenge – if someone cuts off your hand then you must not cut off any more than their hand. Usually a financial payment is made instead.

Forgiveness

Jews believe that they should forgive other people, but they cannot forgive on behalf of others. When he was asked if he could forgive the Nazis for the Holocaust, in which six million Jews were murdered, Rabbi Hugo Gryn said that only G-d could forgive their crimes.

The hope for peace

Judaism believes that most wars are wrong, and people must always seek peace:

> Turn from evil and do good, seek peace and pursue it.
>
> (Psalm 34:15)

This passage shows the hope for peace:

> It will happen in the end of days: The mountain of the Temple of HASHEM will be firmly established as the head of the mountains, and it will be exalted above the hills, and all the nations will stream to it. Many peoples will go and say, 'Come, let us go up to the Mountain of HASHEM, to the Temple of the G-d of Jacob, and He will teach us of His ways and we will walk in His paths.' For from Zion will the Torah come forth, and the word of HASHEM from Jerusalem. He will judge among the nations, and will settle the arguments of many peoples. They shall beat their swords into plowshares and their spears into pruning hooks; nation will not lift sword against nation and they will no longer study warfare.
>
> (Isaiah 2:2–4)

Discussion

Do you think there are occasions when pacifism is not the correct response to a situation?

Activity

Write a sentence describing each type of war in Judaism.

Glossary words

milchemet mitzvah

milchemet reshut

Lex Talionis

Jewish beliefs about the treatment of criminals

Jews believe that criminals must be treated fairly. People accused of a crime should always have a fair trial.

Each of the 36 most serious crimes (including adultery and murder) carried one of four different types of death penalty: stoning, burning, beheading, strangling.

At the time when the Talmud was being written, the rabbis insisted that a criminal must have been warned of the punishment before committing the crime. If all the judges agreed on a verdict, it was thought the verdict was probably wrong. Therefore it was almost impossible to reach a death verdict.

If the death verdict was finally passed, every effort had to be made to have it changed. The accused person was drugged before they were executed. The death penalty was abolished in 30 CE.

For 207 other crimes, criminals were whipped with a maximum of 39 strokes. However, the criminal had to be warned of the punishment, and was given a trial to allow him or her to prove their innocence. A doctor had to agree that the person was well enough to be whipped.

A less severe punishment was **makkat mardut**, or disciplinary lashes.

Jewish responses to social injustice

Jewish teaching about how other people should be treated is very clear:

> When a proselyte (a new convert to Judaism) dwells among you in your land, do not taunt him. The proselyte who dwells

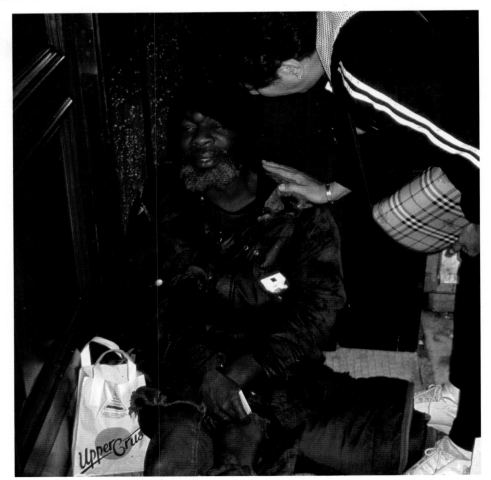

Jews have a duty to care for the poor.

with you shall be like a native among you, and you shall love him like yourself, for you were aliens in the land of Egypt – I am HASHEM your G-d.

(Leviticus 19:33–34)

Many of the prophets wrote about social injustice. The Jews had been badly treated by other peoples. Judaism has always fought against injustice:

Remove from before Me the multitude of your songs, and the music of your lutes I will not hear. Rather, let justice be revealed like water, and righteousness like a mighty stream.

(Amos 5:23–24)

Woe to you who spurn the day of evil, while you convene sessions of injustice; who lie on ivory couches, stretched out on their beds, eating the fattened sheep of the flock and calves from inside the stall; who sing along to the tune of the lute ... who drink wine out of bowls, anoint themselves with choicest oils, and are not pained by the destruction of Joseph.

(Amos 6:3–6)

Jews believe they must try to help anyone or any country in terms of money and development.

Jews should give a tenth of their wealth as **tzedaka** (righteousness). Even the very poorest people should try to give something as tzedaka.

The worst way to give tzedaka is to hand someone the money; the best way is to lend it to them indefinitely and without interest. They hope that the money will help a poor person to become self-supporting.

Discussion

Think about the different purposes of punishment, e.g. revenge, retribution, protection. Which of these do you think is the most important? Why?

Activity

Write a paragraph about how Jewish law tried to give everyone a fair trial.

Glossary words

makkat mardut

tzedaka

Practice GCSE questions

Christianity
(a) Describe Christian beliefs about crime and punishment. (8 marks)
(b) Explain how a Christian might work to make the world a fairer place. (7 marks)
(c) 'It can never be right to fight in a war.' Do you agree? Give reasons to support your answer, and show that you have thought about different points of view. You must refer to Christianity in your answer. (5 marks)

Hinduism
(a) Describe Hindu beliefs about crime and punishment. (8 marks)
(b) Explain how a Hindu might work to make the world a fairer place. (7 marks)
(c) 'It can never be right to fight in a war.' Do you agree? Give reasons to support your answer, and show that you have thought about different points of view. You must refer to Hinduism in your answer. (5 marks)

Islam
(a) Describe Muslim beliefs about crime and punishment. (8 marks)
(b) Explain how a Muslim might work to make the world a fairer place. (7 marks)
(c) 'It can never be right to fight in a war.' Do you agree? Give reasons to support your answer, and show that you have thought about different points of view. You must refer to Islam in your answer. (5 marks)

Judaism
(a) Describe Jewish beliefs about crime and punishment. (8 marks)
(b) Explain how a Jew might work to make the world a fairer place. (7 marks)
(c) 'It can never be right to fight in a war.' Do you agree? Give reasons to support your answer, and show that you have thought about different points of view. You must refer to Judaism in your answer. (5 marks)

Tips

For all four questions

In part **(a)**, you need to show your knowledge of religious beliefs about crime and punishment. You are being tested on your knowledge here, so you do not need to give your own opinions. Try to explain the reasons behind religious beliefs if you can.

In part **(b)**, you need to think of different ways in which followers of the religion you are studying might help to make the world fairer. Perhaps they have started organisations, or there are some which they might join. You could say what these organisations do. You might be able to write about people you have studied who have worked for justice in some way.

In part **(c)**, you are asked to give your own opinion, and to think about different points of view. You should try to include the ways in which religious believers would answer this question. Perhaps they would agree, or disagree, and you need to say why. Maybe they would have different opinions about war, even if they all belong to the same religion. You could explain what these different points of view might be.

Glossary

Christianity

active euthanasia when someone helps a patient to die. This is against the law.

agape a Greek word meaning 'unconditional love'.

altar a table used for sacrifice; in Christianity, it is the table where the Eucharist is celebrated.

Amnesty International an organisation that helps people who have been sent to prison unfairly.

apartheid a system of government in which people of different races are kept apart.

Apostles' creed a statement of Christian beliefs.

ascension when Jesus went into heaven after his resurrection.

Big Bang a huge explosion which many scientists believe marked the beginning of the universe.

Church of England the Anglican Church, which was founded by King Henry VIII.

conscience knowing that something is right or wrong.

conscientious objector someone whose conscience leads them to object to fighting a war.

cosmology the science that includes study of the origins of the universe.

creationist a person who believes that the biblical story of creation, as described in the book of Genesis, is literally true.

Desmond Tutu a black South African Christian who campaigned against racism.

developed countries the more wealthy countries of the world.

developing countries the poorer countries of the world.

Devil a supernatural power of evil, sometimes called 'Satan'.

doctrine of the Trinity the belief that God is 'three persons': the Father, the Son, and the Holy Spirit.

double effect the argument that euthanasia can be allowed if death occurs as a side-effect of a good action, such as pain relief.

ecumenical movement a group of people who work to bring peace between the different Christian groups.

Eucharist also called Holy Communion, Mass, or the Lord's Supper. It is the sacrament celebrating the sacrifice of Jesus and the unity of Christians.

euthanasia when someone is 'helped' to die, without pain, before they would have died naturally.

evangelical the belief that it is important to share one's faith with others.

evolution the process by which living things change through natural selection.

font a special basin which holds the water that is used for baptism.

gospels the four books that tell the story of the life, death and resurrection of Jesus.

Holy Communion *see* Eucharist.

hospice a place where someone who is dying can be nursed and cared for.

hymns prayers that are set to music, for use in worship.

in vitro fertilisation (IVF) a form of fertility treatment in which an egg is fertilised outside the womb.

involuntary euthanasia a form of euthanasia in which the patient cannot or does not ask for help to die.

Just War Theory a set of rules that state when it is 'right' to go to war, or to continue fighting a war.

kingdom of God/kingdom of heaven a time when all people will be ruled by God in a state of unconditional love.

lectern a raised desk on which the Bible is rested when it is being read in church.

liberation theology a Christian movement that helps people to fight against injustice, especially in countries where the government is believed to be unfair to people.

Lord's Prayer the prayer that Jesus taught. It is used regularly by all Christians.

Lord's Supper *see* Eucharist.

Martin Luther King a black Christian civil rights activist.

medical ethics questions of morality that are raised by medical situations.

monogamy a faithful partnership between one man and one woman.

moral evil the kind of evil and suffering that is caused by people doing wrong.

natural evil the kind of evil and suffering that is caused by natural events such as earthquakes and floods.

natural selection the process by which those living things that are best suited to their environment survive and the weaker ones die out.

New Testament the part of the Bible that includes stories of the life of Jesus and teachings about Christian living.

non-violent protest a way of making a point without fighting. Such a protest could be in the form of a march, making a speech, or using a vote.

North–South divide the difference between rich countries (which are mostly in the northern half of the world) and the poorer countries (which are mostly in the southern half of the world). *See* developed countries *and* developing countries.

Old Testament the part of the Christian Bible which also forms the Jewish scriptures. It was written before Jesus was born.

omnipotent all-powerful, able to do anything.

pacifist someone who believes that violence is never justified.

palliative care medical care that involves the control of pain.

parables stories told by Jesus, and by others, which illustrate a moral or religious message.

passive euthanasia a form of euthanasia in which nothing is done deliberately to make death come more quickly, but nothing is done to keep the patient alive. This is not against the law.

prayer communication between God and a person, or people.

pulpit a raised platform on which a speaker stands in church so that he or she is more easily seen and heard.

resurrection raised from the dead to new life.

Roman Catholic Church that part of the Christian Church that is led by the Pope. He is believed to be the successor of Peter, Jesus' disciple.

sacrament a symbolic way of acknowledging the grace of God.

sanctity of life the belief that human life is special to God.

segregation the physical separation of different groups of people, especially black and white people. *See* apartheid.

sermon a speech, usually made in church, in which religious and moral ideas are explained.

Sermon on the Mount a collection of Jesus' teachings about the right way to live. They are set out in Matthew 5–7.

stoup a container for holy water, placed near the entrance of some churches.

Trevor Huddleston a white priest who campaigned against apartheid in South Africa.

voluntary euthanasia a form of euthanasia in which someone asks for help to bring death more quickly.

ॐ Hinduism

ahimsa non-violence, not causing injury or harm to any living creature.

amrit holy water, the drink of immortality.

artha goal of life: wealth, achievement and success.

arti the offering of light to God during worship.

ashramas four stages of life, each with its own code of conduct.

Atman the eternal spirit, or Self.

AUM a sacred and eternal symbol and sound used in meditation and worship. Also known as Om.

avatars appearances of the god Vishnu on the earth, at times of trouble.

Bhagavad Gita 'the song of the Lord', which forms part of the Mahabharata.

bhajan the singing of holy songs during worship.

bhakti loving devotion to God.

brahmacarya one of the four ashramas, or stages of life. Brahmacarya is the first, or 'student', stage.

Brahman God. The one truth, of which all the different deities are aspects.

Brahmins members of the highest, priestly caste.

dalits the oppressed; members of the lowest, 'untouchable' group. *See* harijans.

dana charitable giving.

deities gods and goddesses.

dharma truth, virtue. The right code of conduct appropriate for someone's social status and stage of life.

Ganesha a popular Hindu deity, with an elephant's head. The god of wisdom and the remover of obstacles.

garbha-griha the inner shrine of a mandir, also called a vimana.

Gayatri mantra a prayer to the sun, in the Vedas. It is recited at the beginning and end of every day.

grihastha the second of the traditional stages of life – the householder.

guru a teacher or spiritual guide.

harijans a term invented by Mahatma Gandhi to describe the people who had been known as 'untouchables', or dalits. It means 'children of God'.

havan giving sacred fire to the gods as part of worship.

kama physical pleasure.

karma action, deed. Also the natural law that brings about good results for good deeds, and suffering for bad deeds.

Kshatriyas members of the second, warrior caste.

Lakshmi the goddess of beauty, good luck and prosperity, often shown with a lotus in her hand.

Laws of Manu a code of conduct, traditionally believed to have been written by Manu, the first man.

Mahabharata an epic work of Hindu literature, telling the story of two warring families, and dealing with topics such as dharma, morality and salvation.

mandapa the main hall of a Hindu temple, often with a dome over it.

mandir a Hindu temple.

mantras ways of communicating with God using words repeated as chants and in meditation.

mehndi traditional patterns painted on the body with henna, for decoration.

moksha final freedom from the endless chain of death and rebirth.

murti a statue or picture of a deity, used as a focus for worship and meditation.

Om *see* AUM.

pacifist someone who believes that violence is never justified.

puja an act of worship, a ritual.

Rama a favourite deity of Hinduism, an avatar of the god Vishnu and the hero of the epic tale, the Ramayana.

Ramakrishna Mission a movement that seeks to promote the equality of Hinduism with other world religions, and works for religious tolerance.

Ramayana an epic tale of Rama and his faithful wife Sita. It tells of their exile and adventures and eventual return to the throne.

rebirth (reincarnation) the movement of Atman, the essential Self, from one life at the point of death to the next life at birth.

Rig Veda the oldest religious book known to humanity. It is a collection of sacred hymns.

rishis 'wise people', for example the inspired composers of the Vedas, and others who have taught Hindu wisdom.

samsara the endless cycle of birth, death and rebirth.

sannyasin someone who has reached the fourth stage of life and has renounced worldly possessions to become a homeless wanderer.

Sanskrit the holy language of Hinduism.

sati a practice in which a widow would throw herself onto her husband's funeral pyre. It is now illegal.

Sita a goddess, the wife of Rama. She is a Hindu model of faithfulness and ideal womanhood.

Shiva one of the most important deities of Hinduism: the 'lord of the dance', creator and destroyer.

smriti 'that which is remembered'; traditional Hindu writings that are often very popular but do not have the authority of sruti.

sruti 'that which is heard'. Hindu texts that are believed to have been heard as eternal sounds and recorded in the Vedas.

Sudras members of the fourth, servant caste of Hinduism.

suttee *see* sati.

swastika a Hindu symbol of good luck.

Upanishads sacred Hindu texts which come after the Vedas. They deal with matters of morality and philosophy.

vahana animals that are believed to be 'vehicles' of the gods.

Vaishyas members of the third, professional caste.

vanaprastha someone who has passed the 'householder' stage of life and is ready to renounce the world.

varnas different social classes, believed by Hindus to have been created from the beginning of the world.

Vedas the oldest and most sacred texts of Hinduism. *See* sruti.

vimana the inner shrine of a mandir, where the images of the deities are kept.

 **Islam**

Adhan call to prayer. The Mu'adhin is 'the one who makes the call to prayer'.

Akhirah everlasting life after death – the hereafter.

al-Fatihah the Opener: Surah 1 of the Qur'an. It is recited at least 17 times daily during the five times of Salah. Also known as 'The Essence' of the Qur'an.

al-Janna Paradise.

Al-Mi'raj the ascent of the Prophet Muhammad ﷺ from the earth to Allah in heaven.

Al-Qadr The belief that Allah has already decided what will happen to everyone in the world.

fitrah being born without sin.

Hajj annual pilgrimage to Makkah, which each Muslim must undertake at least once in a lifetime if he or she has the health and wealth. A Muslim male who has completed Hajj is called *Hajji*, and a female, *Hajjah*.

Harb al-Muqadis Holy War.

ibadah all acts of worship, and any action performed with the intention to obey Allah.

'Iblis the Jinn who defied Allah by refusing to bow to Adam (peace be upon him), and later became the tempter of all human beings. Also known as 'Shaytan', meaning rebellious, proud, the devil.

iman faith.

Islam peace attained through willing obedience to Allah's divine guidance.

Jahannam the fires of Hell.

jihad personal individual struggle against evil in the way of Allah. It can also be collective defence of the Muslim community.

Jinn beings (spirits) created by Allah from fire.

Ka'bah a cube-shaped structure in the centre of the grand mosque in Makkah. It is the first house that was built for the worship of the One True God.

khutbah talk delivered on special occasions, as at the mosque on Fridays.

Makkah city where the Prophet Muhammad ﷺ was born, and where the Ka'bah is located.

mala'ikah angels, messengers of Allah.

mihrab niche or alcove in a mosque wall, indicating the Qiblah – the direction of Makkah, towards which all Muslims face to perform Salah.

minaret a tower on a mosque from which the Adhan or call to prayer is made.

minbar rostrum, platform or dais. The stand from which the Imam delivers the khutbah or speech in the mosque or praying ground.

Mujahid the name given to a person who completes jihad.

Qur'an that which is read or recited. The Divine Book revealed to the Prophet Muhammad ﷺ. Allah's final revelation to all people.

Ramadan the ninth month of the Islamic calendar, during which fasting is required from just before dawn until sunset, as ordered by Allah in the Qur'an.

riba interest made on money.

Risalah prophets.

sadaqah charity donation, additional to zakah, which can be given when someone is in need.

Salah communication with, and worship of, Allah, performed in a particular way as taught by the Prophet Muhammad ﷺ, and recited in the Arabic language. The five daily times of Salah are fixed by Allah.

Salat-ul-Jumu'ah Friday prayers at the mosque.

Sawm the time of fasting, from just before dawn until sunset, during the month of Ramadan.

Shahadah declaration of faith, which includes the statement: 'There is no god except Allah, Muhammad ﷺ is the Messenger of Allah'.

Shari'ah Muslim law, which all Muslims should follow. In countries where the government is Muslim, the legal system is based on Shari'ah.

Shaytan another name for 'Iblis.

shirk a sin, as when people believe in anything except Allah, or believe that something is as important as Allah. Shirk in Islam is anything that is forbidden.

Surah division of the Qur'an (there are a total of 114).

tawhid the belief that there is only one god, Allah. Allah created and looks after the universe, and he rules and controls everything that happens.

ummah the world-wide community of Muslims, the nation of Islam.

wudu the ritual washing of hands, mouth, nose, face, arms, head, ears and feet before prayer.

Yawmuddin The Day of Judgement, when everyone will be raised from their graves.

zakah the payment of money to the Muslim community, which purifies the remainder of a person's wealth.

zalim wrongdoing against Allah, other people, or yourself.

Judaism

Adonai Lord.

anti-Semitism persecution of Jews because of their race and religion.

aron hakodesh holy ark: the focal point of the synagogue, containing the Torah scrolls.

bimah platform in the synagogue from which the Torah is read.

challah enriched bread used particularly on Shabbat and during festivals.

chazan leader of reading, singing and chanting in some synagogue services.

Chevra Kadisha the Sacred Burial Society which prepares dead bodies for burial.

covenant an agreement made between G-d and the Israelites.

diaspora the spread of the Jews all over the world.

Final Solution the name given by the Nazis to Hitler's attempt to completely wipe out the Jews during the Second World War (1939–45).

Gan Eden Paradise.

Gehenna Gehinnom, or Hell, where the wicked will be punished.

Gemilut Hasadim 'kind actions' – a form of active Jewish charity.

get divorce document, needed before a person can remarry.

halakhic life walking with G-d, following the Ten Commandments and the 613 mitzvot.

hanukiah nine-branched candlestick used at the festival of Hanukkah.

Hanukkah an eight-day festival of lights to celebrate the re-dedication of the Temple following the Maccabean victory over the Greeks.

HASHEM Lord.

havdalah ceremony marking the end of Shabbat.

Holocaust the systematic murder by the Nazis of six million Jews between 1933 and 1945. *See* Shoah.

huppah canopy under which the bride and groom stand during the wedding ceremony.

Kaddish prayer that is recited publicly by mourners after someone has died.

keriah a tear which people make in their clothes when they hear of a death.

ketubah document that defines rights and duties within Jewish marriage.

Ketuvim 'Writings': the third section of the Tenakh.

kiddushin wedding ceremony.

kosher fit, proper – refers especially to foods permitted by Jewish dietary laws.

Lex Talionis The Law of Retaliation, which limits the amount of revenge that can be taken.

makkat mardut disciplinary lashes used as punishment.

'Master Race' the name given by Hitler to the German people, whom he intended should rule the world.

menorah seven-branched candelabrum which represents the one that was lit daily in the Temple.

mezuzah a scroll placed on doorposts of Jewish homes. It contains a section from the Torah and is often enclosed in a decorative case.

Midrash collection of comments on the Tenakh by various rabbis.

mikveh ritual bath (both the place and the act of bathing) taken by a woman after her monthly period before she can resume normal sexual relations with her husband.

milchemet mitzvah a Holy War, one that is ordered by G-d.

milchemet reshut an optional war – in effect a Just War.

mitzvah commandment (plural *mitvot*), often used to describe good deeds. The Torah contains 613 **mitzvot**.

Nevi'im 'Prophets': the second section of the Tenakh.

niddah laws of purity, which prevent a woman from having sex during her monthly period.

Noachide Code seven laws given to Noah after the flood, which all people should follow. These laws form the foundation for a just society.

pikuakh nefesh 'save a soul': the setting aside of certain laws in order to save a life.

pushke box in which money is collected for charity.

schechitah ritual killing of an animal in a manner that is acceptable to Jews.

scrolls the rolls on which the Torah is written.

Shabbat the day of spiritual renewal and rest. It begins at sunset on Friday, and ends at nightfall on Saturday.

Shema important Jewish prayer that states belief in one G-d. The Shema is found in the Torah.

Sheol a dark place where people go after death and where they stay for eternity.

Sheva Berachos the seven blessings said at a marriage ceremony.

Shoah desolation. The term refers specifically to the suffering experienced during the Holocaust by European Jews at the hands of the Nazis, including the systematic murder of six million Jews between 1933 and 1945.

Talmud the 'Oral Torah', which helps Jews to understand the five books of the 'Written Torah'. The Talmud is a collection of the teachings and explanations of rabbis.

Tenakh the collected 24 books of the Jewish Bible, comprising three sections: the Torah, Nevi'im, and Ketuvim (Te-Na-Kh).

terefah forbidden – the opposite of kosher.

Torah law, or teaching. It is made up of the Five Books of Moses: Genesis, Exodus, Leviticus, Numbers and Deuteronomy, and forms the first part of the Tenakh.

tzedaka righteousness, represented by an act of charity. Jews are expected to give a tenth of their wealth as tzedaka.

yad the pointer used to read scrolls without touching them by hand.

yahrzeit year-time, or anniversary, of a death.

Yom Kippur Day of Atonement: a fast day occurring on the tenth day after Rosh Hashanah.